BIGOTRY
AND
BLOOD

Charles Carlton

BIGOTRY AND

BLOOD
Documents on the Ulster Troubles

Nelson-Hall nh Chicago

Library of Congress Cataloging in Publication Data

Main entry under title:

Bigotry and blood.

  Bibliography: p.
  Includes index.
  1. Northern Ireland—History—Sources.
2. Ireland—History—Sources.   3. Irish question—
Sources.   I. Carlton, Charles.
DA990.U46B42   941.5   76-17018
ISBN 0–88229–278–1 (hardbound)
ISBN 0–88229–469–1 (paperback)

Manufactured in the United States of America

Contents

Acknowledgments

Grateful acknowledgment is made to the following for permission to reprint copyright material: To the British Information Services, Gale Research Company, Mr. R. A. Bruce, and to the Controller of Her Britannic Majesty's Stationery Office for The Downing Street Declaration (Northern Ireland Cmnd 4154). The extracts from Breandan MacGiolla Choille, *Intelligence Notes, 1913-1916*, are reproduced with the permission of the Controller, Stationery Office, Dublin. Prime Minister O'Neill's television speech of 9th December 1968 is reprinted by permission of Faber and Faber Ltd. and Lord O'Neill from *Ulster at the Crossroads*. Acknowledgment must also be made to *Playboy* magazine, C. J. Fallon Ltd., Intercontinental Press, Associated Book Publishers Ltd., the *New Statesman*, Pantheon Books, Walton's Musical Instrument Galleries, and the Puritan Printing Company, Ltd. "On the Irish Parliament" is reprinted from *Swift: Poetical Works*, ed. Herbert Davis, by permission of the Oxford University Press, Oxford. Oliver Cromwell's letter of 17th September 1649 is reproduced from *The Writings and Speeches of Oliver Cromwell*, edited by W. C. Abbott (Cambridge, Mass.: Harvard University Press, 1930), © 1939 by the President and Fellows of Harvard College. Renewed 1967 by Charles C. Abbott.

I would like to thank the staffs of the following libraries for their help: Cambridge University Library, the Library of Congress, Duke University Library, the Folger Shakespeare Library, and the D. H. Hill Library at North Carolina State University. Thanks must also be paid to David C. Bailey, Anthony LeQ. Clayton, and James A. Stewart for several stimulating — and at times vehement — discussions about the Ulster troubles.

Introduction

On the twelfth of August 1969 a group of Ulster Protestants assembled in Londonderry for their annual march commemorating an event that had taken place 290 years before. In 1689 the Catholic forces of King James II had besieged the city for fifteen weeks. At their approach, Robert Lundy, the royal governor, had wished to surrender, the city being weakly defended, short of food, and jammed with refugees. But a group of Protestant "apprentice boys" slammed the city's gates in King James's face and, by committing him to an unsuccessful siege, dashed his chances of regaining the throne. Within a year William of Orange decisively beat James at the Battle of the Boyne, and after the last of James's followers surrendered at Limerick in 1691 the Protestant ascendancy over Britain and Ireland was secure.

To commemorate nearly three centuries of supremacy, on August 12th 1969 Protestants of all ages and from every part of the province had come to Londonderry for their annual apprentice boys' parade. They wore dark Sunday suits and bowler hats, carried rolled umbrellas, and sported orange sashes. Their bands played provocative tunes — some wishing the Pope in hell — and as they marched around the city's walls they derisively tossed pennies into the Bogside, the Catholic ghetto. When the procession reached Waterloo

Street a group of Catholic youths greeted it with catcalls. Stones were thrown, then bricks and bottles.

The apprentice boys' parade often provoked such a fracas. It was almost a tradition. But this time the violence got out of hand and feelings, already raw from over a year of civil rights agitation, broke all restraints. To separate the crowds the police made baton charges, and as they tried to remove hastily thrown up barricades one of their armored vehicles was set afire. By nightfall full-scale rioting developed: petrol bombs and burning cars and buildings illuminated the center of Derry, and the smell of C.S. gas was everywhere. In Dublin, Prime Minister Jack Lynch of the Irish Republic demanded that United Nations troops be sent to Derry to keep the peace. In Belfast, Major Chichester-Clark, Premier of Northern Ireland, told Lynch to mind his own business.

The next day troops were sent into Derry — not the blue helmets of the U.N. but 300 British regulars in full battle dress. By the weekend, 600 more soldiers were patrolling the streets of Belfast, where two days and nights of sectarian rioting had resulted in six dead and 300 wounded.

At first the soldiers brought peace. Catholics welcomed them as protectors from Protestant vigilantes — including the official brand, the B Specials (the reserve police) — and offered the soldiers that deepest-felt British benevolence, cups of tea. But it did not last. Because of the long history of enmity between the British army and Irish nationalists, it could not last. Within months, relations degenerated and the familiar pattern of bombing, shooting, assassination, reprisal and counter reprisal had returned to Ireland.

In 1836 Benjamin Disraeli, later Prime Minister of England, had complained that "Irish history is a vicious cycle of bigotry and blood." In August 1968 the cycle started to turn again, and it is still turning.

The main purpose of this volume is to help readers — especially those in North America — understand the situation in Ulster and, perhaps, gain compassion for all the parties involved. Such an understanding is possible only through a knowledge of Ireland's history and comprehension of the interplay between the past and present.

It is, of course, difficult to appreciate a problem that has yet to be resolved and about which no author can be completely detached. This volume will not ask who is to blame for the present crisis but, instead, what are the various ingredients of the problem and which of the solutions that have been suggested are the fairest and have the best chance of working. To make such an assessment the author and the reader must first define the nature of the conflict. Is it essentially religious or is it prompted by economic considerations? A similar question could be asked of the "black problem" in the United States. Is the Ulster crisis a product of racial bigotry or economic motives? Since the American experience has been very similar to that of Northern Ireland, we will compare the two.

In Northern Ireland the cliché that the past creates the present is particularly true. Today's crisis is the product not just of past events but of people's conceptions — and misconceptions — of them, which, reinforced by stirring songs, annual marches, small but vital details and historically defined tribal areas, produce the current situation. The various groups gain their self-images from the past. Protestant extremists feel that they must live up to the courage displayed by the 36th Red Hand Division at the Somme in 1916 — and may even remember that while the Ulstermen reached their objectives, the British divisions on either flank failed to do so and had to retreat. Some Catholics see themselves as the heirs to "those fearless men and true" who rose in Dublin on Easter Monday, 1916. English soldiers, nurtured on newsreel pictures of the liberating Tommy giving candy to grateful children, are perplexed and angered to find themselves shot at in familiar streets and stoned by English-speaking moppets whose language would make a sergeant-major blush.

Groups also see their adversaries in terms of the past. The Royal Ulster Constabulary consistently refer to civil rights workers or suspected Irish Republican Army (IRA) men as "Fenian bastards." (The Fenians were a nineteenth-century revolutionary group based in the United States.) A few years ago a pop tune in Dublin referred to the British army, which had just been sent to the North, as "Cromwell's men," even though Oliver Cromwell died in 1658.

Although Cromwell, who ruthlessly quelled Ireland in the seventeenth century, has often been blamed as the source of all her troubles, we may trace the roots of the present

crisis, which is perhaps the last great unfinished chapter of
Ireland's history, as far back as 1169, when Earl Robert
FitzStephen led the first English invasion of Ireland. At first
English influence extended only to the Pale, a small district
around Dublin, and by the end of the fifteenth century was
practically extinct. But in the next century the situation
drastically changed:

> Ever since Luther's cruel reformation
> Poor Erin is burthened with tax and taxation,
> The sweet laws of God and land violated,
> Transportation and hanging the pride of our nation.

The Reformation shattered the unity of Christendom,
sparking centuries of religious conflagration, which still
burns in Northern Ireland. England became Protestant and
(perhaps because she did so) Ireland remained Catholic. At
the end of the sixteenth century Queen Elizabeth I felt she
had to conquer her western neighbor for reasons of national
security: geography made Ireland the back door for invasion
of Protestant England by any foreign Catholic army. In the
seventeenth century English and Lowland Scots colonized
Ulster, according the property rights of the natives the same
respect their compatriots gave the American Indians; and by
the end of the century, through a policy of confiscation and
deportation of the native Irish to the west (again like the
Indians) only a ninth of Ireland remained outside Protestant
ownership.

The Penal Laws of the eighteenth century, the short-
lived success of Grattan's Parliament in the 1780s, the
disastrous rebellion of 1798, and the equally unsuccessful Act
of Union two years later further embittered sectarian hatreds.
During the potato famine of the 1840s, one million out of a
population of roughly eight million died of starvation or
disease and another million were forced to emigrate, often
under the most deplorable conditions. This catastrophe was
to the Irish what the concentration camps would be to the
Jews — the holocaust from which their national state would
come.

During the late nineteenth century the movement for
Irish Home Rule grew, winning practically every parliamentary seat in the South, and as its chances of success increased,

so did the opposition of the Northern Unionists, who, with the support of the English Conservative party, were prepared to take their defiance to the point of civil war. In the early twentieth century, Unionists, led by Edward Carson, formed the Ulster Volunteers, a private army, and Nationalists followed suit in the South by creating the Irish Volunteers. With the outbreak of the First World War in 1914, most Irishmen rallied around the British flag. However, the Easter Rebellion of 1916 and the subsequent executions by the British destroyed any consensus, and gradually the British lost control of all of Ireland except the North, to which it granted Home Rule in 1920. Three years of guerrilla war forced the English to recognize the independence of the South, but as a member of the empire.

In 1922 the goal of a united and independent Ireland had not been realized. "This land of ours is still half free/Six counties are under John Bull's tyranny" sang patriots in the South. In the North, where the population was — and still is — two-thirds Protestant and a third Catholic, the majority employed self-government to create a Protestant state. The Unionist party dominated the Stormont, Ulster's parliament — there as far as political power was concerned, no Catholic Irish need apply.

While historical events produced partition and today's sectarian hatreds, popular conceptions of the past have been just as important in maintaining partition and sectarianism as vital issues. Protestants reinforce their tribal loyalties with annual commemorations of the siege of Londonderry: Catholics remind themselves of their unique historical heritage by observing the anniversary of the Easter Rising. Many popular songs recall yesterday's triumphs and the other fellow's perfidy. Thus history ceases to be the record of events and becomes a reservoir for hope and hatred, frustration and self-congratulation. Fancy is far more important than fact. For instance, Protestants celebrate James II's loss at the Boyne as a crashing defeat for the Pope — although in 1690 the Pope sympathized with William of Orange since the Pope was at odds with Louis XIV, James's sponsor, over the rights of the church in France.

The past determines many of the small differences that to an outsider may seem trivial but — like "black," "negro," or "nigra" in America — are code words of tremendous importance. Catholics avoid christening their children William or George; Protestants eschew James or Patrick. Protestants call Ulster's second largest city Londonderry while Catholics still refer to it as Derry — even though James I changed its name three years before Shakespeare died. Indeed, semantic pitfalls are legion, many of them being based on the past. One can say "Ulster," "Northern Ireland," or "the Six Counties" and evoke nuances as different as those implied by "Eire," "the Irish Free State," "Ireland," or "Southern Ireland." Different attitudes are expressed by talking of "the famine" or "the starvation" of the 1840s, or of the "Easter Rising" or "Rebellion."* Because housing and education are largely segregated, one can discover someone's religion simply by asking them where they live or went to school. In Northern Ireland you don't need skin pigmentation to spot the other side.

The historic — almost archaic — nature of the conflict in Northern Ireland makes it hard for outsiders to understand. Congratulating themselves on their religious toleration, they forget that bigotry based on the length of a man's hair, the color of skin, or social class is no less absurd than bigotry determined by the way one worships his Maker.

That outsiders find Ulster's hatreds absurd and irrelevant has in many ways proved to be a blessing. Unlike Southeast Asia, Ulster has not become the cockpit for competing cold war ideologies. Logically, one would expect the IRA, a guerrilla army whose "Official" wing is openly Marxist, to receive support from the Communist world. In fact, most of its outside help has come from Colonel Ghadaffi, the ultra Moslem President of Libya, and from conservative Irish Americans.

While memories of the past — of the famine, say, and hordes of desperate immigrants thronging the ports of the New World — have undoubtedly shaped the attitudes of many Irish Americans, an effort to forget the past has been equally important in influencing British opinion. British schools and universities virtually ignore Irish history, except insofar as it impinges on British politics. This neglect of the

---

* I have chosen between alternatives, including that of "England" and "Britain" on stylistic grounds.

sad story of Britain's dealings with Ireland — always a convenient way of handling the less savory chapters of one's history — means that the average Englishman reacts with angry incomprehension when he reads of yet another outrage across the Irish Sea.

Similarly, English politicians remember only what disastrous effects Irish affairs have had on their history. Events in Ireland precipitated the outbreak of the English Civil War in the seventeenth century, aided the revolutions of the American colonists and the French in the eighteenth, and in modern times have twice split the Conservative party and helped destroy the Liberals. From the Earl of Essex in the sixteenth century to William Gladstone in the nineteenth, Ireland has been the graveyard of English politicians. No wonder that, a few days after the first troops had been sent into Derry in 1969, James Callaghan, the minister responsible for Ireland, privately declared that Britain "on no account wanted to get sucked into the Irish bog."

The British government, nevertheless, was dragged into the "bogs" of Ulster just as reluctantly as the American government a decade before had been drawn into the civil rights struggle of the South. The parallels between the U.S. South and Ulster are considerable: the concept of states' rights or provincial autonomy vis-a-vis Washington or London is powerful, and "exploited minorities" are about a third of the population.* Compared to the nations as a whole, both regions have declined in population and power, are rural, and have low standards of living. From Reconstruction until the 1950s, Washington left the South free to deal with its minority — a policy that London followed with Ulster for half a century after partition. Ulster and the U.S. South also share strong military traditions and have ultra-conservative organizations, such as the Orange Lodges and the Ku Klux Klan. Both are vocal in their patriotism. Edward Carson once vowed to fight Britain to remain British, if necessary, and Southern leaders have defied the government of the United States to protect their particular brand of Americanism. In both regions society and politics are largely

---

*34.9% of Ulster's population is Catholic, compared to 29.5% black in the former Confederate States and 43% in the Deep South, i.e. Alabama, Mississippi, Louisiana, and South Carolina.

deferential, hierarchically structured along vertical lines, and do not have such strong horizontally aligned interest groups as the rest of the nation. In Ulster and the U.S. South, conservative politicians have been able to play upon fear of Catholics, or blacks, to win the votes of Protestant working-men or poor whites, who might otherwise have voted for more liberal candidates.

In the 1950s the Southern status quo broke down, due in part to a gradual improvement of the condition of blacks. A decade later in Ulster, during the premiership of Terence O'Neill, the lot of Catholics improved. The Stormont administration adopted English social security benefits and encouraged the growth of new industries. An influential Catholic middle class developed, many Catholics going to Queen's University, Belfast, where they were influenced by the student movement of the sixties. Using the model and tactics of the American civil rights movement, including the song "We Shall Overcome," Catholics organized to end discrimination. Civil rights, with its associations of Martin Luther King, a Protestant preacher, was respectable, and did not have the tinge of treason that could be attributed to earlier Catholic movements. Televised outrages, such as the police suppression of the Derry civil rights march of October 1968 or the attack on the marchers at Burntollet Bridge in January of the next year, had the same effect on public opinion as the outrages at Selma or Birmingham, Alabama.

But the Southern civil rights movement did not explode into an orgy of sustained violence, as black rioting was mainly confined to Northern ghettos; and the United States government, often prodded by court decisions, granted the movement's demands. Britain does not have so strong a system of judicial review as the United States or so highly developed a concept of constitutional rights. The Supreme Court would never tolerate the Special Powers Act, which, for instance, allows the Northern Ireland government to imprison anyone at will and indefinitely. While the U.S. Constitution guarantees a state the right of self-government, Parliament can easily revoke Ulster's autonomy. But it did not do so until 1972, after three years of violence. The South lacks a tradition of organized black violence, and it has no IRA or neighboring haven that is safe for guerrillas.

However, in Martin Luther King this minority had a moderate leader, the like of which Ulster's Catholics have not produced.

Violence is, of course, difficult to measure. In psychological terms, the threat of violence in Belfast — where troops, searches, barricades, and bombed-out buildings are omnipresent — is far more intense than in any American city. Yet statistics present a very different picture than is gained from one's senses or from the television cameras. During the first six years of "the troubles," 1,000 people died in Northern Ireland; during the single year 1974 in Detroit, which has an equivalent population, 801 people were murdered. If we express violent deaths per 100,000 population, the rates for Northern Ireland are 11.8 in 1971, 40.0 in 1972, 17.0 in 1973, and 9.7 in 1974. Compared to the figures before the troubles (0.3) or for England and Wales (0.7), these rates seem high, yet compared to those in the United States they are not excessive. During 1974 the murder rate for the United States as a whole was 9.26 — for New York 29.4, Washington 38.9, Atlanta 50.8, and Detroit 57.7.

While such statistics might suggest that Americans have a high tolerance for violence, they nonetheless reveal a tragic escalation of violence, which, though declining from a peak in 1972, continues at an alarming rate.

Who, then, was responsible for allowing this situation to develop in Northern Ireland? The British government, for letting Protestants exploit the minority and for not rescinding provincial self-rule sooner? Has the British army behaved with humanity and restraint, or are soldiers, by virtue of the training, incapable of policing hostile communities for sustained periods? Is the Protestant majority really to blame for creating a system of inequality that lacked consensus and, through the Unionists, establishing a one-party state that denied Catholics any hope of achieving anything through the political system? Is the IRA, whose violence has lent credence to Unionist claims that Catholics must be excluded from power as potential traitors, greatly to blame? Certainly its assessment of the North as six "British occupied" counties that are anxious to return to Eire once the Redcoats have been expelled is debatable. Has Southern Ireland, in fostering the Irish language and giving

the Catholic church special privileges and powers, and
allowing the border to become a domestic political football,
done all it could to facilitate reunification?

Another, even more fundamental, question arises. Is the
strife in Ireland basically religious or economic? Does Ulster,
where 64 percent of Protestants attend church at least once a
month and 95 percent of Catholics go to Mass weekly, suffer
from a surfeit of religion and a dearth of Christianity, or is
religion a mask for some other motive?

Perhaps Ulster's Protestants — like poor Southern
whites — are conscious that theirs is the poorest part of the
nation, and to compensate they need some group beneath
them? In the same way, do Catholics need the dream of a free
and united Ireland, won by "the bold brave IRA," to escape
the drabness of their wretched ghettos, where nearly every
other young man is unemployed? But if economics and the
psychological demands of poverty are at the root of the
problem, why should Catholics want to give up Northern
Ireland's living standards and welfare benefits, which are
about a quarter higher than those in the South? Why should
the British government spend roughly £400 million ($960
million) a year more in Ulster than it gets back in taxes? It
could be argued, of course, that the British taxpayer is picking
up the £400 million tab so that capitalists can reap their
profits — and that if much of the British army were not in
Northern Ireland it would be spending badly needed
Deutschemarks in Germany, where it could not train with
real bullets.

Differing answers to all these questions have largely
determined the various solutions suggested in this volume,
ranging from those of Bernadette Devlin and Cathal Goulding to Ian Paisley and R. A. Bruce. In late 1973 many people
felt that the Sunningdale Agreement had the best chance of
restoring peace to Northern Ireland. This agreement, signed
December 9 of that year by the British government of Edward
Heath, the Irish government, and Northern Ireland's political moderates, established a center-based coalition government for the province, founded on the very complex proportional representation elections of the previous summer. The
agreement also paved the way for meetings of a Council of
Ireland in which representatives from both the North and

South would sit, and which one day, perhaps, might form the basis for eventual reunification.

Yet three months later, in the British general election of February 1974, Ulster's Protestant majority overwhelmingly rejected the Sunningdale Agreement, returning to the Westminster Parliament members all but one of whom were opposed to coalition rule. Ulster's Unionist members broke their eighty-year-old alliance with the Conservative party, toppling the government of Edward Heath. The logic of their action is hard to discern for it brought into power a Labor government that is far less sympathetic to the Protestant cause. Several months later, in May 1975, many Protestants demonstrated that the sympathy of the British government was a solace they found neither desirable nor relevant. Late that month an almost complete strike of Protestant workers brought the province to a standstill, toppled the interfaith government Sunningdale so laboriously created, and returned Ulster to direct rule from London.

Since then violence in Ulster has continued, albeit at a reduced rate. The army claims to have the IRA reeling and on the ropes, which would explain that movement's truce of Christmas 1974. Even though the truce is still in effect, and after eight years of fighting the people of Northern Ireland are exhausted, the killing continues, much of it between rival factions of the same faith. On average three or four people die a week as the private armies rebuild their strength. Probably the peace is no more than an IRA-called "time out," rather than the beginning of the end of Ireland's troubles.

After the massive Protestant workers' strike of May 1974, which showed the British that if they worked out a solution acceptable to one side it would be intolerable to the other, Westminster, almost in desperation, proposed a constitutional convention in which the province should solve its own problems. Northern Ireland held elections in the spring of 1975 and the convention met in the summer. To encourage the convention to compromise, the British muttered something about withdrawing their army and subsidies if it could not reach agreement. But such a threat had not the force it once enjoyed. The IRA has always wanted the British out. Some Protestants would welcome the chance granted by the

withdrawal of the army to "sort out the taigs" by launching
a pogrom against the Catholic areas, while even more
Protestants — basically conservative folk — are finding the
link with Britain daily less attractive. They see Britain
becoming increasingly permissive, socialist, inflation ridden,
dominated by trade unions, and with a growing black
population. Indeed if only it could manage to jettison its links
with the Catholic church such Protestants might one day find
the government of the South, a rural, stable conservative
regime, more to their tastes.

It would be ironic if, after so many attempts to unite
Ireland under the red flag of revolution, reunification came
under the banner of reaction. But that seems unlikely. At
present Northern Ireland's future looks bleak. Admittedly
the constitutional convention has lasted longer than many
commentators thought, but there is no sign of its producing
any agreement acceptable to all parties. Worse still — and for
the first time since the troubles began — if the convention
fails Ulster has no more peaceful options left, and could
easily drift into full-scale civil war.

Since the present situation is so fluid any prognostica-
tion about Northern Ireland's future is both risky and likely to
be obsolete before it appears in print. Yet of the future one
thing is certain: like the present it will be shaped by the past.
But whereas knowledge of the past is essential for
understanding the present, it may well be a hindrance in
finding a solution to the present crisis. If the record shows that
all parties are not completely innocent — and there is blame
(and its sequel, revenge) to be accorded to all — a fair and
workable solution may be possible only by forgetting the past.
In other words, Northern Ireland's future may depend on
escaping its history.

I
The
Historical
Background

1.
The Conquest

If the bull or epistle *Laudabiliter* is genuine, it is ironic that England first received authority to conquer Ireland from the Pope. Adrian IV, the only Englishman to occupy the papal throne, granted the bull to Henry II a few years before the first English invasion by Robert FitzStephen in 1169. Later, during the Middle Ages, English influence was confined to the Pale, a small enclave around Dublin, and by the end of the fifteenth century had almost faded away.

THE BULL LAUDABILITER (C. 1154)

Adrian, the bishop, a servant of the servants of God, to his dearest son in Christ Jesus, the illustrious king of England, sends greeting and apostolical benediction. The desire your Magnificence expresses to extend your glory upon earth, and to lay up for yourself in heaven a great reward of eternal happiness, is very laudable and profitable for you, while, as a good catholic prince, you endeavour to enlarge the bounds of the church, to declare the true Christian faith to ignorant and barbarous nations, and to extirpate all evil from the field of the Lord; which the better to perform, you ask the advice and encouragement of the apostolical see. In the accomplishment of this work we trust you will have, by the assistance of God, a success proportioned to the depth of counsel and discretion with which you shall proceed: forasmuch as every thing which takes its rise from the ardour of faith and

4

love of religion is most like to come to a good and happy end. There is indeed no doubt, that (as you yourself acknowledge) Ireland, and all other islands, which Christ, the sun of Righteousness has illumined, and which have received the doctrines of the Christian faith, belong, of right, to the jurisdiction of St. Peter and the most holy Roman church. Wherefore we more gladly sow in them the seed of faith, which is good and agreeable to God, as we know that it will be more strictly required of our conscience not to neglect it. Since then you have signified to us, most dear son in Christ, that you desire to enter into the island of Ireland, in order to subdue the people to the obedience of laws, and extirpate the vices which have there taken root, and that you are also willing to pay an annual pension to St. Peter of one penny from every house therein, and to preserve the rights of the church in that land inviolate and entire, we, seconding your pious and commendable intention with the favour it deserves, and granting a benignant assent to your petition, are well pleased, that for the enlargement of the bounds of the church, for the restraint of vice, the correction of evil manners, the culture of all virtues, and the advancement of the Christian religion, you should enter into that island, and effect what will conduce to the salvation thereof and to the honour of God. It is likewise our desire, that the people of that country should receive you with honour, and venerate you as their master: provided always, that the ecclesiastical rights therein remain inviolate and entire; and reserving to St. Peter and the most holy Roman church the annual pension of a penny from every house. If therefore you think fit to put your design in execution, endeavour studiously to instruct that nation in good morals, and do your utmost, as well personally, as by others whom you know, from their faith, doctrine, and course of life, to be fit for such a work, that the church may there be adorned, the Christian religion planted and made to grow, and whatsoever appertains to the honour of God and the salvation of souls so ordered, as may entitle you to an eternal reward from God, and a glorious name upon earth.

George Lord Lyttleton, *History of the Life of Henry the Second* (London: J. Dodsley, 1772), V, pp. 57–59. *(Note:* As seems appropriate, spelling and punctuation have been modernized in all the documents.)

For the English, the Reformation of the early sixteenth century made the conquest of Ireland more necessary and more difficult. Catholic Ireland became the back door for the invasion of Protestant England. There England's ideological enemies, the Spanish especially, could expect a warm welcome from a Catholic people who hated the English, not only as foreign invaders but as heretics.

As they were to do later with the Indians of North America, the English first used their legal system to try to gain control of Irish land. Through the policy of surrender and regrant, Henry VIII brought Irish chieftains into the English system of feudal tenures. Thus if a chieftain subsequently rebelled, his land would be forfeit to the crown as a traitor's. But his followers refused to recognize such confiscation of land, on which they were usually tenants, since under Irish law the chief had no right to surrender it in the first place.

As the 1542 act proclaiming the kings of England also monarchs of Ireland suggests, the English laid the legal basis for a conquest that had to be consummated in the second part of the sixteenth century by much bloodier means.

SURRENDER AND REGRANT (1541)

First the said MacGilpatrick do utterly forsake and refuse the name of MacGilpatrick, and all claims which he might pretend by the same, and promises to name himself for ever hereafter by such name as it shall please the King's Majesty to give him.

Item, the said MacGilpatrick, his heirs and assigns, and every other of the inhabitants of such lands as it shall please the King's Majesty to give unto him, shall use the English habits and manner, and, to their knowledge, the English language, and they, and every of them, shall to their power bring up their children to the English manner, and the use of the English tongue.

Item, the said MacGilpatrick, his heirs and assigns, shall keep and put such of the said lands as shall be meet for tillage in cultivation and tillage for husbandry, and cause houses to be made and built for such people as shall be necessary for the maintenance thereof.

Item, that the said MacGilpatrick, his heirs and assigns and every of them shall be obedient to the King's Majesty's laws, and answer to His Highness' writs, precepts and commandments, in His Majesty's castle of Dublin, or in any place where his court shall be kept.

Item, that the said MacGilpatrick, his heirs and assigns, nor any of them shall maintain, succour, receive, or to take to sojourn any of the King's enemies, rebels or traitors.

Item, the said MacGilpatrick shall hold his lands by one whole knight's fee.

Signed with MacGilpatrick's mark.

State Papers, Henry the Eighth (London: Record Commission, 1843), III, pp. 291–92.

AN ACT THAT THE KING OF ENGLAND, HIS HEIRS, AND SUCCESSORS BE KINGS OF IRELAND (1542)

Forasmuch as the King our most gracious dread sovereign lord, and his grace's most noble progenitors, Kings of England, have been lords of this land of Ireland, having all manner kingly jurisdiction, power, pre-eminences, and authority royal, belonging or appertaining to the royal estate and majesty of a King, by the name of Lords of Ireland, where the King's majesty and his most noble progenitors justly and rightfully were, and of right ought to be, Kings of Ireland, and so to be reputed, taken, named, and called, and for lack of naming the King's majesty and his noble progenitors, Kings of Ireland according to their said true and just title, style, and name therein, hath been great occasion, that the Irish men and inhabitants within this realm of Ireland have not been so obedient to the King's highness and his most noble progenitors, and to their laws, as they of right and according to their allegiance and bounden duties ought to have been: wherefore at the humble pursuit, petition, and request of the lords spiritual and temporal, and other the King's loving, faithful, and obedient subjects of this his land of Ireland, and by their full assents, be it enacted, ordained, and established by authority of this present Parliament, that the King's highness, his heirs and successors, Kings of England, be always Kings of this land of Ireland, and that his Majesty, his heirs and successors, have the name, style, title, and honor of King of this land of Ireland, with all manner honors, pre-eminences, prerogatives, dignities, and other things whatsoever they be, to the estate and majesty of a King imperial appertaining or belonging; and that his majesty, his heirs and successors, be from henceforth named, called, accepted, reputed, and taken to be Kings of this land of Ireland, to have, hold, and enjoy the said style, title, majesty, and honors of King of Ireland, with all manner pre-eminences, prerogatives, dignities, and all other the premises unto the King's highness, his heirs and successors for ever, as united and knit to the imperial crown of the realm of England.

The Statutes at large passed by the Parliaments held in Ireland (Dublin: Boulter Grierson, 1765), I, 176.

Under Elizabeth the conquest of Ireland was completed. Aside from the expense which cost a parsimonious queen over £2 million, the war was fought with great ferocity. Sir Humphrey Gilbert, Sir Walter Raleigh's half-brother, who later explored the New World, made Irish rebels who wished to surrender walk to his tent through an avenue of heads severed from their less pliant compatriots. In his chronicle John Hooker describes the savagery of the fighting which, as Sir Peter Carew's secretary, he had seen firsthand. To Hooker the Irish were not really people but subhumans who, like "gooks," should be "wasted" at will. Fynes Moryson shared this view of the Irish. He had been secretary to a great soldier, Charles Blount, Lord Mountjoy, Elizabeth's most able and determined general, who completed the conquest of Ireland in 1603 with the fall of Ulster and the surrender of the Earls of Tyrone and Tryconnell.

JOHN HOOKER'S CHRONICLE (1586)

Sir Peter Carew, having had and obtained this victory, and marching in good order, did return with all his company to the town of Kilkenny, every captain and soldier carrying two Gallowglassis axes in his hand, but left the spoil to their followers. Sir Edmund Butler at this instant was not in the camp, but was at his uncle's house at dinner. The townsmen of Kilkenny were very sorry for this the slaughter of so many men. And yet nevertheless not long after, James Fitzmoris came to this town, and besieged it. But the town being well garrisoned with certain soldiers, and they themselves well appointed, did so carefully and narrowly look to themselves, that they defended and kept the town, notwithstanding all his force. But yet the country and other small towns did not so escape, for the county of Waterford, and the Lord Powre, the county of Dublin, and all the country were spoiled, preyed and overrun. And among all others the old Fulco Quimerford a gentleman, of long time servant to three earls of Ormond, was robbed in his house at Callon of two thousand pounds, in money, plate, and household stuff, besides his corn and cattle. When they had taken their pleasure in this country, they went to the county of Wexford, which thing had not lightly been seen before, and at a fair kept then at Enniscorthy, there the soldiers committed most horrible outrages, lamentable slaughters, filthy rapes and deflowering of young women, abusing men's wives, spoiling the town, and slaughtering of the men, and such as did escape the sword were carried captives and prisoners. From hence they went into Ossory and into the Queen's County, and spoiled the country, burned towns and villages, murdered the people, and . . . the most part, if not the whole land, was imbrued and infected with this rebellion.

And here may you see the nature and disposition of this wicked, effrenated [ungovernable], barbarous, and unfaithful nation, who (as Cambrensis wrote of them), they are a wicked and perverse generation, constant always in that they be always inconstant, faithful in that they be always unfaithful, and trusty in that they be always treacherous and untrusty. They do nothing but imagine mischief, and have no delight in any good thing. They are always working wickedness against the good, and such as be quiet in the land. Their mouths are full of unrighteousness, and their tongues speak nothing but cursedness. Their feet swift to shed blood, and their hands imbrued in the blood of innocents. The ways of peace they know not, and in the paths of righteousness they walk not. God is not known in their land, neither is his name called rightly upon among them. Their queen and sovereign they obey not, and her government they allow not: but as much as in them lie do resist her imperial estate, crown, and dignity. It was not much above a year past, that captain Gilbert with the sword so persecuted them, and in justice so executed them, that then they in all humbleness submitted themselves, craved pardon, and swore to be for ever true and obedient: which, so long as he mastered and kept them under, so long they performed it. But the cat was no sooner gone, but the mice were at play; and he no sooner departed from them, but forthwith they skipped out, and cast from themselves the obedience and dutifulness of true subjects. For such a perverse nature they are of, that they will be no longer honest and obedient, than that they cannot be suffered to be rebels. Such is their stubbornness and pride, that with a continual fear it must be bridled; and such is the hardness of their hearts, that with the rod it must be still chastised and subdued. For no longer fear, no longer obedience and no longer than they be ruled with severity, no longer will they be dutiful and in subjection; but will be as they were before, false, truce-breakers and traitorous. Being not much unlike to Mercury called quicksilver, which let it by art be never so much altered and transposed, yea and with fire consumed to ashes; yet let it but rest a while untouched nor meddled with, it will return again to its own nature, and be the same as it was at the first. And even so daily experience teaches it to be true in these people. For withdraw the sword, and forbear correction, deal with them in courtesy, and treat them gently, if they can take any advantage they will surely skip out, and as the dog to his vomit, and the sow to the dirt and puddle, they will return to their old and former insolence, rebellion, and disobedience . . . .

And out of Limerick [the lord justice] marched the tenth of March to Rathkeale, where within one hour the Earl of Ormond came unto him, and there consulted for the manner of the persecution of the enemy. Which when they had agreed upon, they passed the next morning over the bridge of Adare, and by the way they burned and spoiled the country, and went to Rathkeale. Now when they had mended the bridge which the rebels had destroyed, and made passable, they passed over the same into Connilo, where the lord justice and the Earl of Ormond divided their companies, and as they marched they burned and destroyed the country, and they both that night camped within one mile at Kilcoleman. And there it was advertised, that Nicholas Parker, lieutenant to Captain Fenton, coming from Limerick with five horsemen, and three shot, which were of the garrison at Adare, he was set upon at Rathkeale by a hundred traitors, who did discharge sixteen or eighteen shot at him, and sundry darts, before he espied them. But he and James Fenton the captain's brother, and Guidon, so bestirred themselves, that they gave the enemy the repulse, and slew their leader, with five or six others, and so came safe to the camp, but with the hurt of one of their horses.

The soldiers likewise in the camp were so hot upon the spur, and so eager upon the vile rebels, that that day they spared neither man, woman, nor child, but all were committed to the sword. The same day, a soldier of the marshal's encountered with two lusty Kernes [Irish foot soldiers], the one of them he slew, and the other he compelled to carry his fellow's head with him to the camp; which, when he had done, his head also was cut off and laid by his fellow's.

After this followed an extreme famine. And such as whom the sword did not destroy, the same did consume, and eat out; very few or none remaining alive, saving such as dwelt in cities and towns, and such as were fled over into England. And yet the store in the towns was very far spent, and they in distress, albeit nothing like in comparison to them who lived at large. For they were not only driven to eat horses, dogs and dead carrions, but also did devour the carcases of dead men, whereof there be sundry examples. Namely one in the county of Cork, where when a malefactor was executed to death, and his body left upon the gallows, certain poor people secretly came, took him down, and did eat him. Likewise in the bay of Smerwick, or Saint Mary's week, the place which was first seasoned with this rebellion, there happened a ship to be there lost through foul weather, and all the men being drowned, were there cast on land.

The common people, who had a long time lived on limpets, orewads [seaweed] and such shellfish as they could find, and which were now spent, as soon as they saw these dead bodies, they took them up, and most greedily did eat and devour them: and not long after, death and famine did eat and consume them. The land itself, which before those wars was populous, well inhabited, and rich in all the good blessings of God, being plenteous of corn, full of cattle, well stored with fish and sundry other good commodities, is now become waste and barren, yielding no fruits, the pastures no cattle, the fields no corn, the air no birds, the seas (though full of fish) yet to them yielding nothing. Finally, every way the curse of God was so great, and the land so barren both of man and beast, that whosoever did travel from the one end unto the other of all Munster, even from Waterford to the head of Smerwick, which is about six score miles, he should not meet any man, woman, or child, saving in towns or cities; nor yet see any beast, but the very wolves, the foxes, and other like ravening beasts: many of them lay dead being famished, and the residue gone elsewhere. A heavy, but a just judgement of God upon such a Pharoical and stiffnecked people, who by no persuasions, no counsels, and no reasons, would be reclaimed and reduced to serve God in true religion, and to obey their most lawful prince in dutiful obedience; but made choice of a wicked idol, the god Mazim to honor, and of that wicked antichrist of Rome to obey, unto the utter overthrow of themselves and of their posterity.

John Hooker [alias Vowell], "The Chronicles of Ireland," in Ralph Holinshed, *Holinshed's Chronicles of England, Scotland and Ireland* (London: J. Johnson, 1808), VI, pp. 363, 369, 429–30, 459–60.

MOUNTJOY'S CONQUEST OF IRELAND
(c. 1600)

The hearts of the English common soldiers, broken with a current of disastrous successes, he heartened and encouraged by leading them warily, especially in his first actions, being more careful that our men should not be foiled, than the rebels should be attempted with boldness. To this end also, and that he might ever be at hand, as well to encourage and direct them fighting, as to second them by an action dismayed, he bravely adventured his person more than in the opinion of military wise men a general should. My Lord [Mountjoy] himself had his horse shot under him, and I had my thigh bruised with a shot I received in my saddle.

The rebels being swollen to the height of pride by their full numbers, and much more by the continuing success of their actions, he proceeded in like sort with them as formerly with his own men, at the first warily testing them with light skirmishes, yet he so prudently and bravely pursued his attempts, as he still carried what he attempted.

The wise distribution of forces availed him much, for first he planted garrisons upon the chief rebel's counties, and likewise compassed Tyrone on every side with them, which kept the rebels at home so they could not second each other for fear of losing their goods.

And whereas other deputies used to make two or three journeys in a summer against the rebels, and then did lead a great army with them, and whereas this kind of service never took to any good effect, as well as because the bruit [noise] thereof came long before to the rebels, as because the great forces could not long be kept together. So as the rebels hearing the great bruit of such journey took victuals with them for certain days, and assembling themselves together did lie upon the bogs and hard passages, where without danger to themselves they were able to annoy the greatest army that could be led against them. This noble Lord Mountjoy to the contrary, by garrisons keeping them at home, himself kept the field with some thousand foot and two hundred horse, and casting out false reports of them to deceive the rebels, had the opportunity to assail and spoil anyone of the rebels on the sudden.

Again, where other deputies used to assail the rebels only in summertime, this lord prosecuted them mostly in winter, being commonly five days in the week on horseback all winter long. This broke their hearts, for the air being sharp, and they naked, and they being driven from their lodgings into the woods bare of leaves they had no shelter for themselves. Beside that their cattle, giving no milk in winter, were also wasted by driving to and fro. And that they were being thus troubled in seed time they could not sow the ground. And in harvest time both the deputy and the garrisons cut down their corn before it was ripe, so now in wintertime they carried away or burnt all the stores of victuals in secret places whither the rebels had conveyed them.

Again he had special care to cut down and clear the difficult passages that so our forces might with more safety meet together, and upon all occasions second one another.

For protections and pardons he never received any to any mercy, but such as had drawn blood on their fellow rebels, and were themselves made so poor that there was small danger of their relapse.

By these counsels this worthy lord restored the declining state of Ireland from the desperate terms wherein he found it.

Fynes Moryson, *The Rebellion of the High Earle of Tyrone and the Appeasing thereof* (London, 1617), pp. 49-50.

2.
The Colonization

Once the English had completed their conquest of Ireland their next problem was holding it. They used the flight of the Earls of Tyrone and Tryconnell to the Continent in 1607, and the abortive rebellion of Cahir O'Doherty the next year, as an excuse to confiscate most of Ulster. James I gave much of this land to "undertakers," such as Hugh Montgomery, James Hamilton, and the city of London, and they in return agreed to bring over English and Scots settlers — leaving the remnants, usually bogs and waste, for the native Irish. The English accorded the rights of the Irish as scant respect as they were later to show the American Indians. Indeed, the conquest and colonization of Ireland was in many ways a prelude to that of the New World.

CONDITIONS FOR THE COLONIZATION OF ULSTER (1608)

Whereas the greatest part of the six counties in the province of Ulster in the realm of Ireland, namely Armagh, Tyrone, Coleraine, Donegal, Fermanagh and Cavan, being escheated and come to the crown, have been surveyed, and the survey thereof transmitted and presented unto his Majesty. Upon view whereof his Majesty out of his princely bounty, not respecting his own profit, but the public peace and welfare of that kingdom, by the civil plantation of those unreformed and waste counties, is graciously pleased to distribute the said lands to such of his subjects as well of Great Britain as of Ireland, as being of merit and ability shall seek the same, not only to benefit themselves, but to do service to the crown and the commonwealth. And for as much as many persons are ignorant of the conditions whereupon his Majesty is pleased to grant the said lands. . . . It is thought convenient to declare and publish to all his Majesty's subjects the several quantities of the portions that shall be distributed, the several sorts of undertakers, the manner of allotment, the estates, the rents, the tenures, with other articles to be observed as well on his Majesty's behalf, as on the behalf of the undertakers in manner and form following.

First the proportion of lands to be distributed to undertakers shall be of three different quantities, consisting of sundry parcels or precincts of land. . . . The first, or least, proportion to contain such or so many of the said parcels as shall make up 1,000 English acres at the least, and the second, or middle, proportion to contain such or so many of the said parcels as shall make up 1,500 English acres at the least. And the last, or greatest, proportion to contain such or so many of the said parcels as shall make up 2,000 English acres at the least. To every of which proportion shall be allowed such quantity of bog or wood as the country shall conveniently afford.

Secondly the persons of the undertakers of the several proportions shall be of three sorts:

1. English and Scottish as well servitors [servants] as others, who are to plant their portions with English or inland Scottish inhabitants.

2. Servitors in the kingdom of Ireland, who may take mere Irish, English or inland Scottish tenants at their choice.

3. Natives of Ireland who are to be made freeholders.

Thirdly his Majesty will reserve unto himself that appointment of what county every undertaker shall have his portion. But to avoid emulation and controversy, which would arise among them if every man should choose the place where he would be planted, his Majesty's pleasure is that the sites or places of their portions in every county shall be distributed by lot.

Articles concerning the English and Scottish undertakers who are to plant their portions with English or inland Scottish tenants:

(1) His Majesty is pleased to grant estates in fee farm to them and their heirs.

(2) They shall yearly yield to his Majesty for every proportion of 1,000 acres £5 6s. 8d. . . . . But none of the said undertakers shall pay any rent until the expiration of the first two years, except the natives of Ireland, who are not subject to the charge of transportation. . . .

(4) Every undertaker of the greatest proportion of 2,000 acres shall within two years of his letter's patent build thereupon a castle with a strong court or bawn [fortified cattle pen] about it. And every undertaker of the second, or middle, proportion of 1,500 acres shall within the same time build a stone or brick house thereupon, with a strong court or bawn about it. And every undertaker of the least proportion of 1,000 acres shall within the same time make thereupon a strong castle or bawn at the least. And all the said undertakers shall draw their tenants to build houses for themselves and their families, near the principal castle, house or bawn for their mutual defence and strength. And they shall have sufficient timber, by the assignment of such officers as the Lord Deputy and Council of Ireland shall appoint, out of his Majesty's woods in that province, for the same buildings, without paying anything for the same during the said two years. . . .

(5) The said undertakers, their heirs and assignees, shall have ready in their houses at all times a convenient store of arms wherewith they may furnish a competent number of able men for their defence, which may be viewed and mustered every half year according to the manner of England.

(6) Every of the said undertakers, English or Scottish, before the sealing of his letter's patent, shall take the oath of supremacy [to the King of England], either in the Chancery of England or Ireland, or before the commissioners to be appointed for the establishing of the plantation, and shall also conform themselves in religion according to his Majesty's laws [i.e., be Protestants].

(7) The said undertakers, their heirs and assignees, shall not alienate or devise their portions, or any part thereof, to the mere

Irish, or such person who will not take the oath which the said undertakers are bound to take. . . .

(8) Every undertaker shall within two years after the date of his letter's patent plant or place a competent number of English or inland Scottish tenants upon his portion. . . .

(9) Every undertaker for the space of five years next after the date of his letter's patent shall be resident in person himself upon his portion, or place some such other person thereupon as shall be allowed by the state of England or Ireland, who shall be likewise resident there during the said five years, unless by reason of sickness or other important cause he be licensed by the Lord Deputy and Council of Ireland to be absent himself for a time.

(10) The said undertakers shall not alienate their lands during five years next after the date of their letter's patent. . . . But after the said five years they shall be at liberty to alienate to all persons except the mere Irish and such persons who will not take the oath, which the said undertakers are to take aforesaid.

(11) The said undertakers are to have power to erect manors, to hold courts baron twice every year, to create tenures. . . .

Articles concerning the Irish natives who shall be admitted to be freeholders:

(1) They shall have their estates in fee farm.

(2) They shall pay the yearly rent of £10. 13s. 14d. for every portion of 1,000 acres. . . . And they shall pay no rent for the first year.

(3) For their tenures they shall hold as the other undertakers respectively according to their portions, with the provision of forfeiture if they enter into actual rebellion.

(4) They shall inhabit their lands and build their castles, houses, and bawn within two years as the former undertakers.

(5) They shall make certain estates for years or for lives to their under-tenants, and they shall take no Irish exactions.

(6) They shall use tillage and husbandry in the manner of the English pale.

Certain general propositions to be noted by undertakers of all sorts:

(1) That there shall be commissioners appointed for the setting forth of the several proportions, and for the ordering and settling of the plantation according to such instructions as shall be given to them by his Majesty in that behalf.

(2) That all the said undertakers shall by themselves, or by such as the states of England or Ireland shall allow, attend the said commissioners in Ireland, at or before midsummer next, to receive such directions touching their plantations as shall be thought fit.

(3) That every undertaker, before the sealing of his letter's patent, shall enter into bond or recognisance with good sureties to his Majesty's use . . . in this manner: *viz*, the undertakers of the greatest proportion to become bound in £400, in the middle proportion in £300, of the least proportion in £200.

(4) That in every of the said counties there shall be a convenient number of market towns and corporations erected for the habitation and settling of tradesmen and artificers, and that there shall be one free school at least appointed in every county for the education of youth in learning and religion.

(5) That there shall be a convenient number of parishes and parish churches with sufficient incumbents in every county, and that the parishioners shall pay all their tithes in kind to the incumbents of the said parish churches.

A collection of such orders and conditions as are to be observed by the undertakers upon the distribution and plantation of the escheatted lands in Ulster (London, 1608).

By 1641 the colonization of Ulster seemed to be a very great success. Nearly 120,000 English and Scots had settled there (twice as many as had gone to America), and in April of that year the government could congratulate itself that the "plantations have certainly kept the peace and encouraged the growth of the Protestant religion."

It spoke too soon. Within six months Ulster's dispossessed Catholics rose in revolt, demanding the end of English oppression. Stories of the atrocities and outrages of their rising, which were greatly magnified during their passage across the Irish Sea, horrified the English public, who learned of them in pamphlets such as the following.

THE REBELLION OF 1641

There was one of the Rebels called William Rafter, that was taken by Colonel Carot Topey, who discovered this plot, and confessed that the said hill was all undermined, and that there was 100 barrels of powder in the Vault, and their purpose was, that if they could take Athy and the Castle, then they knew that when the King's Forces came to Dublin they would immediately move that way, because by that place they should be much strengthened, and to come to them the way doth lie directly over the said Hill, Rockoll, and with the said powder in the hill, they had determined to blow them up as they passed by.

And he discovered, moreover, that M. Ochashen of Azabe in the Queen's County, about 20 miles from Athy, and 8 miles from the Fort of Leix, together with Sir Florence Fitz-Patrick of Castle-town, should have come by night with 5000 armed men to the Fort of Leix, and lie as soldiers that were to ward, the Papists within had agreed, and were appointed, to let in a certain Company of the Rebels appointed for that purpose to burn and batter down the Town.

Hereupon Captain Picket went forth to meet that company with 500 men who fell upon them, and slew 3 or 400 of the Rebels, and the rest fled into the woods.

Himself sustained the loss of 60 men, slain and dangerously hurt.

The said Rebels did rove extraordinary up and down in Ireland, on Thursday, the 3 of December, 1641, and did them much hurt in divers places of the Country. They came to the town of Rockoll spoken of before, on the same day. The Rebels had a pair of Bag-Pipes which played before them as they marched, which played exceeding loud, which the town hearing, rose to meet them, and at the town's end saluted them, and made them great entertainment, and joined themselves with them by an oath.

Afterwards they went to the aforesaid English inhabitants, William Clarke, and there they slew him, his wife, children, and family, 7 persons in number, of whom they left not one alive, but cruelly murdered them. From thence they marched to the Nassey, that is about 5 miles, a Town of Irish inhabitants, also they did go to the house of an English man, called Henry Orell, where they slew his wife . . . her daughter in the most barbarous manner that ever was known, . . . and mangled her body in pieces without pity or Christianity.

From thence they marched next day toward Athy, which is 10 miles from the Nassey, towards which place, having marched about a mile from the Nassey aforesaid, they came to the Town of Pickingell, a Town inhabited of English, where they fell upon the inhabitants thereof, and slew them in a cruel manner, without mercy to the number of above 20 families, men, women and children. One woman, above the rest, they hanged at her own door with her children, by the hair of the head, and afterwards burned up the whole Town with fire.

Having made that place desolate, they marched the next day forward as before, and having marched some three miles further, they, came to an English man's house, where first they slew the man at the door, and afterwards they entered the house where they found the woman and her maid brewing; for it was an Ale house where they brewed their own drink. The maid they took, and . . . they threw her into the boiling Caldron, or pan of wort, that was then over the fire; and her Mistress they slew and cut off her head; and afterwards fired the house.

"Treason in Ireland for blowing up of the King's English Forces with 100 Barrells of Gunpowder, with the names of the Chief Agents; and the manner of the Discovery, December 10. With a plot discovered at Athy. Sent into England by Mr. Hierome, Minister of God's Word, 1641," in Thomas Fitzpatrick, *The bloody bridge, and other papers relating to the insurrection of 1641* (Dublin: Sealy, Bryers and Walker, 1903), pp. 75–77.

> On reading of such wickedness, all Englishmen agreed that an army had to be raised to punish the rebels. They could not, however, agree whether the King or Parliament should appoint the commanders of this army, the most powerful force in the realm. This issue turned the quarrel between Charles I and Parliament, which had originally stimulated the Irish rebellion, into a civil war that plagued England, Scotland, and Ireland for more than a decade. But the war did not slacken England's thirst for revenge.

Rebels, such as Lord Maguire, were callously executed.
Oliver Cromwell used the atrocities of 1641 to justify his
massacre of the garrisons of Drogheda and Wexford eight
years later, and Parliament used the events of 1641 to
vindicate passage of the 1652 Act of Settlement that confis-
cated the lands of any Irishman even remotely connected
with the rebellion, condemned many of them to death, and
ordered the rest, on pain of execution, to be deported west to
the province of Connaught. "To Hell or Connaught" was
the alternative offered by English Protestants who could not
envisage Catholics going anywhere but to perdition in the
next life.

The Civil War and Cromwellian confiscations deci-
mated Ireland. At least 6,000 Catholics lost their land,
ammounting to 55 percent of the island's total area; 40,000
Irishmen fled into exile; 100,000 were transported virtually as
slaves to the Americas: and one contemporary estimated that
out of a total population of a million and a half, 600,000
Irish men, women, and children perished.

REVENGE: THE EXECUTION OF AN IRISH REBEL (1644)

On Thursday, February 20th, the Lord Maguire was drawn
upon a sledge from the Tower of London, through the city unto
Tyburn, which being come and the cart set ready, he kneeled
upon the sledge and prayed for some time, after which the Sheriff
spoke to him as follows:

Sheriff Gibbs: My Lord Maguire, it is now the last
declaration you are like to make in the world. Here you stand
justly condemned to be executed for a very heinous crime. . . .
Sir, we desire you to express your sense of these very horrid
actions. . . .

Maguire: I have but a short time. Do not trouble me.

Sheriff Gibbs: Sir, it is best that I trouble you that you may
not be troubled for ever.

Maguire: Sir, trouble me not. I have but a little time to spend.

Sheriff Gibbs: Sir, I shall give you as much time after as you shall spend to give satisfaction to the people. . . .

Maguire: I beseech you. Do not trouble me.

Sheriff Gibbs: I have told you I would give you as much time afterwards as I shall take up.

Maguire: I am not disposed to give you any account.

Dr. Sibbalds [a Protestant minister]: If the blood of one man, of Abel, cried to heaven for vengeance, how much more shall the blood of many thousands. Oh, give glory to God by the confession of your sins. . . .

Maguire: Pray give me leave to pray.

Dr. Sibbalds: Give glory to God that your soul may not be presented to God with the blood of so many thousand people.

Sheriff Gibbs: Who were actors or plotters with you, or gave you any commission?

Maguire: For God's sake leave me that I may depart in peace.

Dr. Sibbalds: There is no dissembling now. You are within a few minutes to be presented before the tribunal of that great judge, who will reward every man according to their deeds. . . .

Maguire: I am not of the same religion with you. . . .

Dr. Sibbalds: I beseech you, my lord, in the name of God to discover the truth.

Maguire: What will you have me speak?

Sheriff Gibbs: What inducements moved you to it?

Maguire: All I said in my examinations are true. All I said is right. I beseech you let me depart in peace. . . .

Sheriff Gibbs: Sir, will you die like a stock [fool]? Will you go to hell without mercy and not acknowledge your sorrow for that foul crime?

Dr. Sibbalds: Do you think a Jesuit will pardon you when you will not confess? . . .

Maguire: I beseech you gentlemen, let me have a little time to say my prayers.

Sheriff Gibbs: Sir, if you answer ingeniously to those questions we shall ask you, you shall have time afterwards. Whether you do account the shedding of protestants' blood to be a sin or not? And whether do you desire pardon of God for that sin?

Maguire: For Jesus Christ, I beseech you to give me a little time to prepare myself.

Sheriff Gibbs: Have pity on your own soul.

Maguire: For God's sake, have pity on me and let me say my prayers.

Sheriff Gibbs: I say the like to you in relation to your own soul whether do you think the massacre of so many thousand protestants was a good act? For Jesus Christ's sake have pity on your own soul.

Maguire: Pray let me have a little time to say my prayers.

Sheriff Gibbs: So much good blood spilt and spent by you, and yet no remorse. . . .

Maguire: I do beseech all the catholics that are here to pray for me. I beseech God to have mercy upon my soul. . . .

After this the executioner did his office.

The Last Speeches and Confessions of the Lord Maguire: The Irish Rebell that was hanged at Tyburne and drawne and quartered on Thursday last, the 20th of February, 1644 (London, 1644).

REVENGE: THE MASSACRE OF THE GARRISON OF DROGHEDA (1649)

For the Honourable William Lenthall, Esquire, Speaker of the Parliament of England: These

SIR,

Your Army being safely arrived at Dublin; and the enemy endeavouring to draw all his forces together about Trim and Tecroghan (as my intelligence gave me); from whence endeavours were used by the Marquis of Ormond to draw Owen Roe O'Neal with his forces to his assistance, but with what success I cannot yet learn, I resolved, after some refreshment taken for our weather-beaten men and horses, and accommodations for a march, to take the field. And accordingly, upon Friday the 30th of August last, rendezvoused with eight regiments of foot and six of horse and some troops of dragoons, three miles on the north side of Dublin. The design was, to endeavour the regaining of Tredah; or tempting the enemy, upon his hazard of the loss of that place, to fight.

Your Army came before the town upon Monday following, where having pitched, as speedy course was taken as could be to frame our batteries, which took up the more time because divers of the battering guns were on shipboard. Upon Monday the 9th of this instant, the batteries began to play. Whereupon I sent Sir Arthur Ashton, the then Governor, a summons to deliver the town to the use of the Parliament of England. To the which I received no satisfactory answer, but proceeded that day to beat down the steeple of the church on the south side of the town, and to beat down a tower not far from the same place, which you will discern by the chart enclosed.

Our guns not being able to do much that day, it was resolved to endeavour to do our utmost the next day to make breaches assaultable, and by the help of God to storm them. The places pitched upon were that part of the town-wall next a church called St. Mary's, which was the rather chosen because we did hope that if we did enter and possess that church, we should be the better able to keep it against their horse and foot until we could make way for the entrance of our horse, which we did not conceive that any part of the town would afford the like advantage for that purpose with this. The batteries planted were two: one was for that part of the wall against the east end of the said church, the other against the wall on the south side. Being somewhat long in battering, the enemy made six retrenchments: three of them from the said church to Duleek Gate, and three from the east end of the church to the town-wall and so backward. The guns, after some two or three hundred shot, beat down the corner tower, and opened two reasonable good breaches in the east and south wall.

Upon Tuesday the 10th of this instant, about five o'clock in the evening, we began the storm, and after some hot dispute we entered about seven or eight hundred men, the enemy disputing it very stiffly with us. And indeed, through the advantages of the place, and the courage God was pleased to give the defenders, our men were forced to retreat quite out of the breach, not without some considerable loss; Colonel Cassell being there shot in the head, whereof he presently died, and divers officers and soldiers, doing their duty, killed and wounded. There was a tenalia [small fort] to flanker the south wall of the town, between Duleek Gate and the corner tower before mentioned, which our men entered, wherein they found some forty or fifty of the enemy, which they put to the sword. And this [tenalia] they held, but it being without the wall, and the sally-port through the wall into that tenalia being choked up with some of the enemy which were killed in it, [it] proved of no use for our entrance into the town that way.

Although our men that stormed the breaches were forced to recoil, as before is expressed, yet, being encouraged to recover their loss, they made a second attempt, wherein God was pleased [so] to animate them that they got ground of the enemy, and by the goodness of God, forced him to quit his entrenchment. And after a very hot dispute, the enemy having both horse and foot, and we only foot, within the wall, they gave ground, and our men became masters both of their retrenchments and the church; which indeed, although they made our entrance the more difficult, yet they proved of excellent use to us, so that the enemy could not annoy us with their horse, but thereby we had advantage to make good the ground, that so we might let in our own horse, which accordingly was done, though with much difficulty.

The enemy retreated, divers of them, into the Mill-Mount: a place very strong and of difficult access, being exceedingly high, having a good graft [moat], and strongly palisaded. The Governor, Sir Arthur Ashton, and divers considerable Officers being there, our men getting up to them, were ordered by me to put them all to the sword. And indeed, being in the heat of action, I forbade them to spare any that were in arms in the town, and, I think, that night they put to the sword about 2,000 men, divers of the officers and soldiers being fled over the bridge into the other part of the town, where about one hundred of them possessed St. Peter's church-steeple, some the west gate, and others a strong round tower next the gate called St. Sunday's. These being summoned to yield to mercy, refused, whereupon I ordered the steeple of St. Peter's Church to be fired, where one of them was heard to say in the midst of the flames: "God damn me, God confound me; I burn, I burn."

The next day, the other two towers were summoned, in one of which was about six or seven score; but they refused to yield themselves, and we knowing that hunger must compel them, set only good guards to secure them from running away until their stomachs were come down. From one of the said towers, notwithstanding their condition, they killed and wounded some of our men. When they submitted, their officers were knocked on the head, and every tenth man of the soldiers killed, and the rest shipped for the Barbadoes. The soldiers in the other tower were all spared, as to their lives only, and shipped likewise for the Barbadoes.

I am persuaded that this is a righteous judgement of God upon these barbarous wretches, who have imbrued their hands in so much innocent blood, and that it will tend to prevent the effusion of blood for the future, which are the satisfactory grounds to such actions, which otherwise cannot but work remorse and regret.

And now give me leave to say how it comes to pass that this work is wrought. It was set upon some of our hearts, that a great thing should be done, not by power or might, but by the Spirit of God. And is it not so clear? That which caused your men to storm so courageously, it was the Spirit of God, who gave your men courage, and took it away again; and gave the enemy courage, and took it away again; and gave your men courage again and therewith this happy success. And therefore it is good that God alone have all the glory.

Your most humble servant,

OLIVER CROMWELL.

Dublin,
Sept. 17, 1649

W. C. Abbott, ed., *The Writings and Speeches of Oliver Cromwell* (Cambridge, Mass.: Harvard University Press, 1937–47), II, pp. 125–30.

REVENGE: "TO HELL OR CONNAUGHT" (1652)

Whereas the Parliament of England, after the expense of much blood and treasure for suppression of the horrid rebellion in Ireland, have by the good hand of God upon their undertakings, brought that affair to such an issue, as that a total reducement and settlement of that nation may, with God's blessing, be speedily effected, to the end therefore that the people of that nation may know that it is not the intention of the Parliament to extirpate that whole nation, but that mercy and pardon, both as to life and estate, may be extended to all husbandmen, ploughmen, labourers, artificers, and others of the inferior sort, in manner as is hereafter declared; they submitting themselves to the Parliament of the Commonwealth of England, and living peaceably and obediently under their government; and that others also of higher rank and quality may know the Parliament's intention concerning them, according to the respective demerits and considerations under which they fall; be it enacted and declared by this present Parliament, and by the authority of the same, that all and every person and persons of the Irish nation, comprehended in any of the following qualifications, shall be liable unto the penalties and forfeitures therein mentioned and contained, or be made capable of the mercy and pardon therein extended respectively, according as is hereafter expressed and declared; that is to say

I. That all and every person and persons, who at any time before the tenth of November, 1642 (being the time of the sitting of the first General Assembly at Kilkenny in Ireland), have contrived, advised, counselled, promoted, or acted, the rebellion, murders, or massacres done or committed in Ireland, which began in the year 1641; or have at any time before the said tenth day of November, 1642, by bearing arms, or contributing men, arms, horse, plate, money, victual, or other furniture or hablements of war (other than such which they shall make to appear to have been taken from them by mere force and violence), aided, assisted, promoted, acted, prosecuted, or abetted the said rebellion, murders, or massacres, be excepted from pardon for life and estate.

II. That all and every Jesuit, priest, and other person or persons who have received orders from the Pope or See of Rome, or any authority derived from the same, that have any ways contrived, advised, counselled, promoted, continued, countenanced, aided, assisted, or abetted; or at any time hereafter shall any ways contrive, advise, counsel, promote, continue, countenance, aid, assist, or abet the rebellion or war in Ireland, or any the murders or massacres, robberies, or violences committed against the Protestants, English, or others there, be excepted from pardon for life and estate. . . .

IV. That all and every person and persons (both principals and accessories) who since the first of October, 1641, have or shall kill, slay, or otherwise destroy any person or persons in Ireland, which at the time of their being so killed, slain, or destroyed, were not publicly entertained and maintained in arms as officers or private soldiers, for and on behalf of the English against the Irish; and all and every person and persons (both principals and accessories) who since the said first day of October, 1641, have killed, slain, or otherwise destroyed any person or persons entertained and maintained as officers or private soldiers, for and on behalf of the English against the Irish (the said persons so killing, slaying, or otherwise destroying, not being then publicly entertained and maintained in arms as officer or private soldier under the command and pay of the Irish nation against the English), be excepted from pardon for life and estate.

V. That all and every person and persons in Ireland, that are in arms or otherwise in hostility against the Parliament of the Commonwealth of England, and shall not within eight and twenty days after publication hereof by the Commissioners for the Parliament, or Commander-in-Chief, lay down arms and submit to the power and authority of the said Parliament and Commonwealth as the same is now established, be excepted from pardon for life and estate.

VI. That all other person and persons (not being comprehended in any of the former qualifications) who have borne command in the war of Ireland against the Parliament of

England, or their forces . . . be banished during the pleasure of the Parliament of the Commonwealth of England, and their estates forfeited and disposed of as followeth, viz. that two-third parts of their respective estates be had, taken, and disposed of for the use and benefit of the said Commonwealth; and that the other third part of their said respective estates or other lands, to the proportion and value thereof (to be assigned in such places in Ireland, as the Parliament, in order to the more effectual settlement of the peace of this nation, shall think fit to appoint for that purpose) be respectively had, taken, and enjoyed by the wives and children of the said persons respectively.

VII. That the Commissioners of Parliament and Commander-in-Chief have power to declare, that such person or persons as they shall judge capable of the Parliament's mercy (not being comprehended in any of the former qualifications), who have borne arms against the Parliament of England or their forces, and have laid down arms, or within eight and twenty days after publication hereof by the Commissioners for the Parliament, and the Commander-in-Chief, shall lay down arms and submit to the power and authority of the said Parliament and Commonwealth, as the same is now established (by promising and engaging to be true to the same), shall be pardoned for their lives, but shall forfeit their estates to the said Commonwealth, to be disposed of as followeth, viz. two-third parts thereof (in three equal parts to be divided) for the use, benefit, and advantage of the said Commonwealth, and the other third part . . . by the said persons, their heirs or assigns respectively.

VIII. That all and every person and persons of the Popish Religion, who have resided in Ireland at any time from the first day of October, 1641, to the first of March, 1650, and have not manifested their constant good affection to the interest of the Commonwealth of England (the said persons not being comprehended in any of the former qualifications), shall forfeit one-third part of their estates in Ireland to the said Commonwealth, to be disposed of for the use, benefit, and advantage of the said Commonwealth; and the other two-third parts of their respective estates or other lands, to the proportion or value thereof, to be assigned in such place in Ireland, as the Parliament, for the more effectual settlement of the peace of that nation, shall think fit . . . provided that this shall not extend to make void the estates of any English Protestants, who have constantly adhered to the Parliament. . . . Nevertheless it shall be in the power of the Parliament, or their Commissioners, if they see cause, to transplant such persons from the respective places of their usual habitation or residence, into such other places within that nation, as shall be judged most consistent with public safety, allowing them such proportion of land or estate in the parts to which they shall be transplanted, as they had or should have enjoyed of their own other where, in case they had not been so removed.

"An Act for the Settlement of Ireland" (12 August 1652), in S. R. Gardiner, ed., *The Constitutional Documents of the Puritan Revolution, 1628–1660* (Oxford: Clarendon Press, 1906), pp. 394–99.

> Although the Protestant conquest of Ireland was virtually complete by 1660, the events by which Protestants choose to commemorate their triumph took place twenty-eight years later. During the Glorious Revolution of 1688 a group of English aristocrats deposed James II for trying to return Britain to Catholicism and invited William, Prince of Holland, and his wife Mary, James's daughter, to invade England and take the throne. The next year James landed in Ireland to establish a base for the reconquest of England; but he failed because he could not capture Londonderry and because William decisively beat him on July 12, 1690, at the Battle of the Boyne.
>
> The defenders of Londonderry held out with great fortitude, believing, as their preachers told them, that theirs was God's work. Their governor was George Walker, a Protestant minister, who soon after the siege was killed at the Battle of the Boyne. Rowland Davies, chaplain to one of William's regiments, described this decisive battle. Perhaps Davies (whose journal reveals an inordinate concern for his stomach) drank to the Williamite toast, celebrating the completeness of the Protestant victory over Catholic Ireland. Over the centuries William of Orange became a folk hero — almost a saint — to Ulster's Protestants, who still tell of a foreigner who asked an old man who King Billy was, "Away," the Protestant sage replied, "and read your Bible!"

THE SIEGE OF LONDONDERRY (1689)

April 17th. Upon the news of King James' army being on their march to Londonderry, Colonel Lundy, our governor, thought fit to call a council . . . accordingly they meet and with other gentlemen equally unacquainted with the condition of the town or the inclination and resolution of the people, they make this following order . . . That considering the present circumstances of affairs, and the likelihood that the enemy will soon possess themselves of this place, it is thought most convenient that the principal officers shall privately withdraw themselves, as well for their own preservation, as in hopes that the inhabitants by a timely capitulation may make terms better with the enemy. . . .

April 19th. The garrison, seeing that they were deserted and left without a governor, and having resolved to maintain the town and to defend it against the enemy, they considered of some person they could have confidence in to direct them in the management of this affair, and unanimously resolved to choose Mr. Walker [the diarist] and Major Baker. . . .

April 21. The enemy placed a demi-culverin [light cannon] . . . they played at the houses in the town, but did little or no mischief only to the market house. This day our men sallied out, as many as pleased . . . they killed above 200 of the enemy's soldiers, besides Maumont, the French general. . . .

April 23. The besiegers placed four demi-culverins in the lower end of Mr Strong's orchard . . . these played incessantly, hurt several people in the houses, battered the walls and garrets so that none could lodge safely above stairs. . . .

April 25. They placed their mortar-pieces in the said orchard, and from thence played a few small bombs, which did little hurt to the town, all of them lighting in the streets except one which killed an old lady in a garret. . . .

June 4. This night the enemy from Strong Orchard play their bombs, which were 273 pounds weight apiece, and contained several pounds of powder in the shell. They ploughed up our streets and broke down our houses, so that there was no passing in the streets nor staying within doors, but all flock to the walls and remotest parts of town, where we continued very safe, while many of our sick were killed, not being able to leave their houses. . . . Their bombs were some advantage to us on one account, for being under great want of fuel, they supplied us plentifully from the houses they threw down and the timber they broke for us.

June 7. Three ships came up to Colmore Fort and fired at the castle and attempted coming up the river. But one of them unfortunately ran aground, and lay some time at the mercy of the enemy's shot, and so much on her side she could not make any return. But at length, with some pleasure, we saw her get off, and, as we believed, without much loss or damage.

June 15. . . . The enemy now begin to watch us more narrowly. They raise batteries opposite the ships, and line both sides of the river with great numbers of fire locks. They draw down their guns to Charles Fort, a place of some strength upon the narrow part of the river, where the ships were to pass. Here they contrived to place a boom of timber joined by iron chains and fortified by a cable 12 inches thick. . . .

July 2. The enemy drive the poor protestants according to their threats under our wall, protected and unprotected, men, women and children, and under great distress. Our men at first did not understand the meaning of such a crowd, but fearing that they might be enemies fired upon them. We were troubled when we found the mistake, but it supported us to a great degree when we found that none of them were touched by our shot, which by the direction of providence (as if every bullet had its commission what to do) spared them, and found out and killed three of the enemy that were some of those who drove the poor people into so great danger. . . .

July 27. The garrison is reduced to 4,456 men and under the greatest extremity for want of provision, which does appear by this account taken by a gentleman of the garrison of the price of our food. Horse flesh sold for 1/6d per pound. A quarter of dog, 5/6d, fattened by eating the bodies of the slain Irish. A dog's head, 2/6d. A cat, 4/6d. A rat, 1/-. A mouse, 6d. We were under so great necessity that we had nothing left unless we could prey upon one another. A certain fat gentleman conceived himself in the greatest danger, and fancying that several of the garrison looked at him with a greedy eye, thought fit to hide himself for three days. Our drink was nothing but water, which we paid very dear for, and could not get without great danger. . . .

July 30. About an hour after sermon, being in the midst of great extremity we saw some ships in the Lough make towards us. . . . The enemy fired most desperately upon them from the fort of Colmore and both sides of the river, and they made sufficient returns and with the greatest bravery. The *Mountjoy* made a little stop at the boom, occasioned by her rebound after striking and breaking it, so that she was run aground. . . . At length the ships got to us, to the unexpressable joy and transport of our distressed garrison, for we only reckoned on two days life, and had only nine lean horses left, and among us all one pint of meal to each man. . . . This brave undertaking, added to the great success God had blessed us in all our attempts, so discouraged the enemy that on the last of July they ran away in the night time. . . .

Rev. George Walker, *A true account of the siege of London-Derry* (1st ed. 1689), ed. Philip Dwyer (London: E. Stock, 1893), pp. 15–16, 18, 22, 25–27, 36–38.

THE BATTLE OF THE BOYNE
(1 July 1690)

June 29th. At two in the morning we decamped, and marched to Ardee; by the way two men were hanged, one for deserting, the other for betraying some of our men to the enemy. In the afternoon I read prayers and preached in the field on Psalm cxviii. 15.

June 30th. At two in the morning we decamped again, and marched toward Drogheda, where we found King James encamped on the other [side] of the Boyne; we drew up all our horse in a line opposite him within cannon-shot, and as His Majesty [William] passed our line they fired six shot at him, one whereof fell and struck off the top of the Duke of Wurtemberg's pistol, and the whiskers off his horse, and another tore the King's coat on the shoulder. We stood open during at least twenty shot, until, a man and two horses being killed among the Dutch guards, we all retired into a trench behind us, where we lay safe while much mischief was done to other regiments, and in the evening drew off and encamped behind the hill.

July 1st. About six in the morning the Earl of Portland marched up the river almost to the bridge of Slane, with the right wing, consisting of twenty-four squadrons of horse and dragoons and six regiments of foot, and at two fords we passed the river where there were six squadrons of the enemy to guard the pass; but, at the first firing of our dragoons and three pieces of cannon that marched with us, they all ran away, killing nothing but one of our dragoon's horses. As soon as we passed the river, we saw the enemy marching towards us, and that they drew up on the side of a hill in two lines, the river on their right, and all their horse on the left wing; their foot appeared very numerous, but in horse we far exceeded. Whereupon the Earl of Portland drew us up also in two lines, intermixing the horse and foot by squadron and battalion, and sent away for more foot to enforce us; and thus the armies stood for a considerable time, an impassable bog being between them. At length six regiments of foot more joined, and we altered our line of battle, drawing all our horse into the right wing; and so outflanking the enemy we marched round the bog and engaged them, rather pursuing than fighting them, as far as Duleek. In the interim Count Solmes with the foot forced the pass under our camp and marched over the river with the blue Dutch regiment of guards; no sooner were they up the hill but the enemy's horse fell on them, ours with the King being about half a mile lower passing at another ford. At the first push the first rank only fired and then fell on their faces, loading their muskets again as they lay on the ground; at the next charge they fired a volley of three ranks; then, at the next, the first rank got up and fired again, which being received by a choice squadron of the enemy, consisting mostly of officers, they immediately fell in upon the Dutch as having spent all their front fire; but the two rear ranks drew up in two platoons and flanked the enemy across, and the rest, screwing their swords into their muskets, received the charge with all imaginable bravery and in a minute dismounted them all. The Derry regiment also sustained them bravely, and as they drew off maintained the same ground with a great slaughter. His Majesty then came up and charged at the head of the Enniskilling horse, who deserted him at the first charge, and carried with them a Dutch regiment that sustained them; but the King's blue troop of guards soon supplied their place, and with them he charged in person and routed the enemy, and coming over the hill near Duleek appeared on our flank, and, being not known at first, made all our forces halt and draw up again in order, which gave the enemy time to rally also, and draw up on the side of the hill, a bog and river being between us, and then they fired two pieces of cannon on us, but did no mischief; but, as soon as our foot and cannon came up, they marched on, and we after them, but, our foot being unable to march as they did, we could not come up to fight again, but, the night coming on, were forced to let them go; but had we engaged half an hour sooner, or the day held an hour longer, we had certainly destroyed that army.

Journal of the Very Rev. Rowland Davies, ed. R. Caulfield (London: Camden Society, 1857), pp. 122-24.

A PROTESTANT TOAST (1690)

The glorious, pious and immortal memory of the great and good King William, not forgetting Oliver Cromwell, who assisted in redeeming us from popery, slavery, arbitrary power, brass money, and wooden shoes. May we never want a Williamite to kick the arse of a Jacobite! And a fart for the Bishop of Cork! And he that won't drink this, whether he be priest, bishop, deacon, bellows-blower, gravedigger, or any other of the fraternity of the clergy, may a north wind blow him to the south, and a west wind blow him to the east! May he have a dark night, a lee shore, a rank storm, and a leaky vessel to carry him over the River Styx! May the dog Cerberus make a meal of his rump and Pluto a snuffbox of his skull! May the devil jump down his throat with a red-hot harrow, and with every pin tear out a gut, and blow him with a clean carcase to hell! Amen!

M. J. MacManus, *Irish Cavalcade, 1550-1850* (London: Macmillan, 1939), pp. 64-65.

3.
The Protestant
Hegemony

To consolidate their victory of the Glorious Revolution, Protestants passed a set of laws, known as the Penal Laws, that deprived Catholics of their civil rights, making them, at best, ninth or tenth class citizens. These laws were intended to force propertied Catholics either to convert or to be dragged down to the level of the poor and exploited Irish. Thus Ireland's Parliament became the emasculated tool of London that Jonathan Swift, Dean of St. Patrick's Cathedral, Dublin, so scathingly described.

AN ACT TO PREVENT THE FURTHER GROWTH OF "POPERY" (1703)

Whereas divers emissaries of the church of Rome, popish priests, and other persons of that persuasion, taking advantage of the weakness and ignorance of some of her Majesty's subjects, or the extreme sickness and decay of their reason and senses, in the absence of friends and spiritual guides, do daily endeavour to persuade and pervert them from the protestant religion, to the great dishonour of Almighty God, the weakening of the true religion, by His blessing so happily established in this realm, to the disquieting the peace and settlement, and discomfort of many particular families thereof . . . And whereas many persons so professing the popish religion have it in their power to raise divisions among protestants, by voting in elections for members

of Parliament, and also have it in their power to use other ways
and means tending to the destruction of the protestant interest in
this kingdom: for remedy of which great mischiefs, and to prevent
the like evil practices for the future, be it enacted by the Queen's
most excellent Majesty . . . That if any person or persons from
and after the twenty fourth day of March, in this present year of
our Lord one thousand seven hundred and three, shall seduce,
persuade, or pervert any person or persons professing, or that
shall profess, the protestant religion, to renounce, forsake, or
abjure the same, and to profess the popish religion, or reconcile
him or them to the church of Rome, then and in such
case . . . shall for the said offences, being thereof lawfully
convicted, incur the danger and penalty of premunire, mentioned in the statute of premunire made in England in the sixteenth year of the reign of King Richard the second. And if any
person or persons being a papist, or professing the popish
religion, shall from and after the said twenty fourth day of March
send, or cause, or willingly suffer, to be sent or conveyed any child
under the age of one and twenty years, except sailors, ship-boys,
or the apprentice or factor of some merchant in trade of merchan-
dise, into France, or any other parts beyond the seas, out of her
Majesty's dominions, without the special licence of her Majesty,
her heirs or successors, or of her or their chief governor or
governors of this kingdom, and four or more of her or their privy
council of this realm, under their hands in that behalf first had
and obtained, he, she, and they, so sending or conveying, or
causing to be sent or conveyed away, such child, shall incur the
pains, penalties, and forfeitures mentioned in an act made in the
seventh year of his late Majesty King William, entitled, An act to
restrain foreign education . . . .

    II. That where any of the judges of her Majesty's courts of
Queen's-bench, Common pleas, or barons of the Exchequer, or
any two of the justices of the peace of any county of this
kingdom, shall have reasonable cause to suspect that any such
child, except before excepted, and also except such child or
children as shall be sent abroad with such licence as aforesaid, has
been sent abroad into foreign parts, he and they are hereby
required and directed to convene the father or mother, or such
other relation, guardian, or other person or persons, as had the

tuition, education, or care of the said child, and shall require him, her, or them, to produce or bring before him or them the said child within two months. . . .

III. And to the end that no child or children of popish parent or parents, who have professed or embraced, or who shall profess or embrace, the protestant religion, or are or shall be desirous or willing to be instructed and educated therein, may in the lifetime of such popish parent or parents, for fear of being cast off or disinherited by them, or for want of a fitting maintenance or future provision, be compelled and necessitated to embrace the popish religion, or be deterred or withheld from owning and professing the protestant religion: be it further enacted by the authority aforesaid, That from and after the said twenty fourth day of March one thousand seven hundred and three upon complaint in the high court of Chancery by bill founded on this act against such popish parent, it shall and may be lawful for the said court to make such order for the maintenance of every such protestant child . . . suitable to the degree and ability of such parent. And in case the eldest son and heir of such popish parent shall be a protestant, that then from the time of the enrolement in the high court of Chancery of a certificate of the bishop of the diocese, in which he shall inhabit, testifying his being a protestant, and conforming himself to the [Anglican] Church of Ireland as by law established, such popish parent shall become, and shall be, only tenant for life of all the real estate. . . .

IV. And that care may be taken for the education of children in the communion of the Church of Ireland as by law established; be it enacted by the authority aforesaid, that no person of the popish religion shall or may be guardian unto, or have the tuition or custody of, any orphan, child or children, under the age of twenty one years; but that the same, where the person having or entitled to the guardianship of such orphan, child or children, is or shall be a papist, shall be disposed of by the high court of Chancery to some near relation of such orphan, child or children, being a protestant. . . .

VI. And be it further enacted . . . that every papist, or person professing the popish religion, shall from and after the said twenty fourth day of March be disabled, and is thereby made incapable, to buy and purchase either in his or in their own name, or in the name of any other person or persons to his or her use, or in trust for him or her, any manors, lands, tenements, or hereditaments, or any rents or profits out of the same, or any leases or terms thereof, other than any term of years not exceeding thirty-one years. . . .

XVII. And be it further enacted . . . that all and every such person and persons, that shall be admitted, entered, placed, or taken into any office or offices, civil or military, or that shall receive pay, salary, fee, or wages belonging to or by reason of any office or place of trust, by reason of any patent or grant from her Majesty, or that shall have command or place of trust from or under her Majesty, or any of her predecessors or successors, or by her or their authority, or by authority derived from her or them, within this realm of Ireland, after the first day of Easter-term aforesaid, shall take the said oaths and repeat the said declaration, and subscribe the said oaths and declaration, in one of the said respective courts in the next term, or at the general quarter-session for that county, barony, or place where he or they shall reside, next after his or their respective admittance or admittances into any such office . . . and all and every such person or persons so to be admitted as aforesaid, shall also receive the sacrament of the Lord's supper according to the usage of the Church of Ireland, within three months after his or their admittance. . . .

XXIV. And for the preventing papists having it in their power to breed dissension amongst protestants by voting at elections of Members of Parliament; be it further enacted . . . that from and after the twenty fourth day of March 1703 no freeholder, burgess, freeman, or inhabitant of this kingdom, being a papist or professing the popish religion, shall at any time hereafter be capable of giving his or their vote for the electing of knights of any shires or counties within this kingdom, or citizens or burgesses to serve in any succeeding Parliament. . . .

The Statutes at large passed in the Parliaments held in Ireland (Dublin: Boulter, Grierson, 1765), IV, pp. 12–30.

ON THE IRISH PARLIAMENT (1730)

Ye paultry underlings of state,
Ye senators, who love to prate;
Ye rascals of inferior note,
Who, for a dinner, sell a vote;
Ye pack of pensionary Peers,
Whose fingers itch for poets ears;
Ye bishops far remov'd from saints;
Why all this rage? Why these complaints?
Why against Printers all this noise?
This summoning of blackguard boys?
Why so sagacious in your guesses?
Your effs and tees, and arrs, and esses?
Take my advice; to make you safe,
I know a shorter way by half.
The point is plain: Remove the cause;
Defend your liberties and laws.
Be sometimes to your country true.
Have once the public good in view:
Bravely despise Champagne at Court,
And chuse to dine at home with Port:
Let Prelates, by their good behaviour,
Convince us they believe a Saviour;
Nor sell what they so dearly bought,
This country, now their own, for nought.
Ne'er did a true satyric muse
Virtue or innocence abuse;
And 'tis against poetic rules
To rail at men by nature fools.

Jonathan Swift, in *Swift: Poetical Works*, ed. Herbert Davis
(London: Oxford University Press, 1967), pp. 427-28.

In the eighteenth century all Irishmen suffered from English oppression. Over 100,000 Catholics, known as "the Wild Geese," fled abroad to fight in the armies of England's enemies. As many Protestants emigrated from Ulster to the American colonies because England excluded them, as Presbyterians, from the privileges of the established Church of Ireland and used the Navigation Acts to destroy their industries whenever they threatened English economic interests.

The American and French revolutions also gave Protestants and Catholics the opportunity to come together in movements such as the United Irishmen (whose constitution bears echoes of the Declaration of Independence) to win concessions from the English. During the 1780s London lost the right to veto legislation passed by the Dublin Parliament. But as the bloody rebellion of 1798 showed, sectarian unity was short lived. By brutally suppressing the peasant armies of Catholic "croppies" (so called from the shortness of their hair) which were led by parish priests such as Father Murphy, Ireland's Protestants demonstrated that they would rather be exploited by the English than lose the opportunity to oppress their Catholic compatriots. And on both sides the balladers ensured that the hatreds engendered in 1798 would not soon be forgotten.

The Constitution of the United Irishmen (1797)

In the present Era of Reform, when unjust Governments are falling in every Quarter of Europe; when religious Persecution is compelled to abjure her Tyranny over Conscience; when the Rights of Men are ascertained in Theory, and that Theory substantiated by Practice; when Antiquity can no longer defend absurd and oppressive Forms against the common Sense and common Interests of Mankind; when all Governments are acknowledged to originate from the People, and to be so far only obligatory as they protect their Rights and promote their Welfare: we think it our Duty as Irishmen to come forward, and state what we feel to be our heavy Grievance, and what we know to be its effectual Remedy: We have no National Government; we are ruled by Englishmen and the Servants of Englishmen, whose Object is the Interest of another Country, whose Instrument is Corruption, and whose Strength is the Weakness of Ireland, and these Men have the whole of the Power and Patronage of the Country as Means to seduce and subdue the Honesty of her Representatives in the Legislature. Such an extrinsic Power acting with uniform Force, in a Direction too frequently opposite to the true Line of our obvious Interests, can be refitted with Effect solely by Unanimity, Decision and Spirit in the People; Qualities which may be exerted most legally, constitutionally and efficaciously by that great Measure, essential to the Prosperity and Freedom of Ireland, — an equal Representation of all the People in Parliament.

Impressed with these sentiments, we have agreed to form an Association, to be called The Society of United Irishmen, and we do pledge ourselves to our country, and mutually to each other, that we will steadily support, and endeavour by all due Means to carry into Effect the following Resolutions:

1st. Resolved, that the Weight of English Influence in the Government of this Country is so great as to require a cordial Union among all the People of Ireland, to maintain that Balance which is essential to the Preservation of our Liberties and Extension of our Commerce.

2d. That the sole constitutional Mode by which this Influence can be opposed is by a complete and radical Reform of the Representation of the People in Parliament.

3d. That no Reform is practicable, efficacious or just, which shall not include Irishmen of every religious Persuasion.

The Journals of the House of Commons of the Kingdom of Ireland (Dublin: Abraham Bradley, 1753–1800), XVII, appendix p. 888.

A "United Irish" Manifesto (1798)

TO THE UNITED IRISHMEN

COUNTRYMEN,

No Moment was ever so awful to Ireland as the present one — Liberty or Slavery is now before us. That the Decision is in your Hand, I am well assured. Glorious Prospect! The People of Ireland are UNITED. Shew the pitiful Tyrants who calumniate you — Shew Europe — Shew the World that you are a Band of Brothers, actuated by a Sense of Honour, Virtue and Patriotism — Shew an Example of the Effects of your Principles in Armagh. The Hills and Valleys which were lately stained with blood, are now covered by the real Spirit of the Gospel, and Peace, and Love, and Charity, and Union reign in the Hearts of IRISHMEN! — Look at this, ye Traducers, ye Dividers, ye Devourers of Ireland. Yes, thank Heaven, we are UNITED, and that our Enemies know right well. Let not the honest Indignation of your virtuous Souls provoke you to a Word or an Action unworthy of your Country or your Cause, when you hear yourselves termed "a Nest of execrable and infamous Traitors." You must learn to smile at the impotent Attacks of malignant Despair.

Look at the Map, says a Ministerial Character, and you will find that Ireland must belong to England or France. What Occasion to look at the Map, or why employ the Word must? But, if this be the Decree of Fate for Ireland, let it be done with Unanimity, with Love, and with Power; let no internal Broils, no local Situations, no religious Opinions, ever provoke an IRISH-MAN to spill the Blood of an Irishman. . . .

Signed: AN IRISHMAN.

The Journals of the House of Commons of the Kingdom of Ireland (Dublin: Abraham Bradley, 1753–1800), XVII, appendix p. 892.

"FATHER MURPHY OF THE COUNTY WEXFORD," A CATHOLIC SONG OF 1798

At Boulavogue, as the sun was setting
O'er the green May meadows of Shelmalier,
A rebel band set the heather blazing,
And brought the neighbours from far and near.
Then Father Murphy, of old Kilcormack,
Spurred up the rocks with a warning cry —
"Arm! Arm!" he cried, "for I've come to lead you —
Now priest and people must fight or die."

He led us on 'gainst the coming soldiers,
And the cowardly Yeomen we put to flight;
Down at the Harrow, the Boys of Wexford
Showed Bookey's regiment how men could fight!
Look out for hirelings, King George of England,
Search every kingdom that breeds a slave!
For Father Murphy, of the County Wexford,
Sweeps o'er the earth like a mighty wave!

We took Camolin and Enniscorthy,
And Wexford storming, drove out our foes;
'Twas at Slieve Kiltha our pikes were reeking
With the crimson stream of the beaten Yeos.
At Tubberneering and Ballyellis
Full many a Hessian lay in his gore!
Ah, Father Murphy, had aid come over,
A green flag floated from shore to shore!

At Vinegar Hill, o'er the pleasant Slaney,
Our heroes vainly stood back to back,
And the Yeos at Tullow took Father Murphy,
And burned his body upon the rack.
God give you glory, brave Father Murphy,

And open heaven to all your men;
The cause that called you may call tomorrow
In another war for the Green again.

George Zimmerman, ed., *Songs of Irish Rebellion* (Hatboro,
Pa.: Folklore Associates, 1967), pp. 290–91.

"CROPPIES LIE DOWN,"
A PROTESTANT REPLY

In the County of Wexford these rebels did rise,
All brave Orange-men they swore they'd sacrifice;
They thought that our army they'd suddenly beat,
But we boldly attacked them, and made them retreat.
Chorus:
Derry down, down, Croppy lie down.

On Vinegar Hill these rebels encamped,
They thought that their numbers our army would damp;
But we boldly attacked them and forced them to yield,
And five hundred Croppies lay dead on the field.

The bold General Dundas is a man of great might,
He attacked the Croppies just by the day-light;
He threw up his bomb-shells and bullets so fast,
That put the damned Croppies to flight at the last.

Colonel Campbell, commanding the first light brigade,
He forced the hill when the attack it was made,
And planted his cannon in such a fine spot,
That made the wild Croppies to curse his grape shot.

These rebels the country they thought to seduce—
They sent bold McManus with a flag of truce;
They thought that the army good terms would give,
But their answer was — "Croppies, we won't let you
live!"

Then Esmond, Kay, with Harvey and Hay,
Unto General Moore was given up next day;
They were tried by Courtmartial, who quickly them
slew,
So there was an end to the blood-thirsty crew.

George Zimmerman, ed., *Songs of Irish Rebellion* (Hatboro,
Pa.: Folklore Associates, 1967), pp. 308-9.

After the rebellion of 1798 even the English realized that
all was not well with Ireland and that reforms were necessary. So two years later they passed the Act of Union,
pressuring the Dublin Parliament into dissolving itself in
return for representation in London. At first Catholics were
not allowed to vote in parliamentary elections, and even
though in 1827 Daniel O'Connell forced the English to
enfranchise Catholics, few of them accepted the legitimacy of
the United Kingdom Parliament: within half a century most
were determined the union must be broken.

The great famine of the 1840s was the turning point in
modern Irish history. For Ireland the introduction of the
potato had been a "green revolution" enabling it to double
its population in a century. But when this single staple crop
failed, catastrophe was inevitable. English politicians, nurtured on the *laissez-faire* teachings of the Manchester School
of economists, did little to relieve the starving Irish — much
less, to be sure, than they would have done had famine raged
back home in Manchester. Out of a population of over 8
million, the famine killed a million Irish and drove as many
to emigrate, mostly to the United States, where, as one of the
refugees put it, "the queen's writ did not run."

QUAKER REPORTS ON CONDITIONS IN
THE WEST OF IRELAND (1846-1847)

Boyle, 5th of 12th Month, 1846
In this place, the condition of the poor previously to their
obtaining admission into the work-house is one of great distress;

many of them declare that they have not tasted food of any kind for forty-eight hours; and numbers of them have eaten nothing but cabbage or turnips for days and weeks. This statement is corroborated by the dreadfully reduced state in which they present themselves; the children especially being in a condition of starvation, and ravenous with hunger. Last year there were no such cases as these; the poor coming into the work-house then from the ·pressure of temporary difficulties, and remaining there a comparatively short time.

Carrick-on-Shannon, 6th of 12th Month, 1846

At this place our first visit was to the poor-house; and as the Board of Guardians were then sitting for the admission of applicants, a most painful and heart-rending scene presented itself; poor wretches in the last stage of famine imploring to be received into the house; women who had six or seven children begging that even two or three of them might be taken in, as their husbands were earning but 8d. per day; which, at the present high price of provisions, was totally inadequate to feed them. Some of these children were worn to skeletons, their features sharpened with hunger, and their limbs wasted almost to the bone. From a number of painful cases, the following may be selected. A widow with two children, who for a week had subsisted on one meal of cabbage each day: these were admitted into the poor-house, but in so reduced a state, that a.guardian observed to the master of the house, that the youngest child would trouble them but a very short time. Another woman with two children, and near her confinement again, whose husband had left her a month before to seek for work, stated that they had lived for the whole of this week upon two quarts of meal and two heads of cabbage. Famine was written in the faces of this woman and her children. In reply to a question from William Forster, the guardians expressed their opinion that these statements were true. Of course, among so many applicants as there were in attendance (110), a great number were necessarily refused admittance, as there were but thirty vacancies in the house. The guardians appeared to exercise great discrimination and impartiality in the selection of the most destitute objects; but some of those who were rejected were so far spent, that it is doubtful if they would all reach their homes alive, as several of them had to walk five or six Irish miles. . . .

Belmullet, County of Mayo,
16th of 3rd Month, 1847

. . . And now language utterly fails me in attempting to depict the state of the wretched inmates. I would not willingly add another to the harrowing details that have been told; but still they are the FACTS of actual experience, for the knowledge of which we stand accountable. I have certainly sought out one of the most remote and destitute corners; but still it is within the bounds of our Christian land, under our Christian government, and entailing upon us — both as individuals and as members of a human community — a Christian responsibility from which no one of us can escape. My hand trembles while I write. The scenes of human misery and degradation we witnessed still haunt my imagination, with the vividness and power of some horrid and tyrannous delusion, rather than the features of a sober reality. We entered a cabin. Stretched in one dark corner, scarcely visible, from the smoke and rags that covered them, were three children huddled together, lying there because they were too weak to rise, pale and ghastly, their little limbs, on removing a portion of the filthy covering, perfectly emaciated, eyes sunk, voice gone, and evidently in the last stage of actual starvation. Crouched over the turf embers was another form, wild and all but naked, scarcely human in appearance. It stirred not, nor noticed us. On some straw, soddened upon the ground, moaning piteously, was a shrivelled old woman, imploring us to give her something — baring her limbs partly, to show how the skin hung loose from the bones, as soon as she attracted our attention. Above her, on something like a ledge, was a young woman, with sunken cheeks, — a mother I have no doubt, — who scarcely raised her eyes in answer to our enquiries, but pressed her hand upon her forehead, with a look of unutterable anguish and despair. Many cases were widows, whose husbands had recently been taken off by the fever, and thus their only pittance, obtained from the public works, was entirely cut off. In many the husbands or sons were prostrate under that horrid disease, — the results of long-continued famine and low living, — in which first the limbs, and then the body, swell most frightfully and finally burst. We entered upwards of fifty of these tenements. The scene was invariably the same, differing in little but the numbers of the sufferers or of the groups occupying the several corners within. The whole number was often not to be distinguished, until, — the eye having adapted itself to the darkness — they were pointed out, or were heard, or some filthy bundle of rags and straw was perceived to move. Perhaps the poor children presented the most piteous and heart-rending spectacle. Many were too weak to stand, their little limbs attenuated, — except where the frightful swellings had taken the place of previous emaciation. Every infantile expression had entirely departed; and in some, reason and intelligence had evidently flown. Many were remnants of families, crowded together in one cabin; orphaned little relatives, taken in by the equally destitute; and even strangers; for these poor people are kind to one another to the end. In one cabin was a sister, just dying, lying by the side of her little brother, just dead. I have worse than this to relate, but it is useless to multiply details, and they are in fact unfit. They did but rarely complain. When we enquired what was the matter, the answer was alike in all, — "Tha shein ukrosh," — indeed the hunger. We truly learned the terrible meaning of that sad word, *ukrosh* . . . !

Transactions of the Central Relief Committee of the Society of Friends during the Famine in Ireland in 1847 (Dublin: Hodges and Smith, 1852), pp. 145-46, 163-64.

"THE EMIGRANT'S FAREWELL TO DONEGAL" (C. 1846)

Good people on you I call, give ear to those lines you soon
    shall hear,
Caus'd me to weep deprived of sleep for parting from my
    relations dear;
My hardships here I can't endure, there's nothing here but
    slavery,
I will take my lot and leave this spot and try the land of
    liberty.

Farewell dear Erin, fare thee well, that once was call'd the
   Isle of Saints,
For here no longer I can dwell, I'm going to cross the
   stormy sea,
For to live here I can't endure, there's nothing here but
   slavery,
My heart's oppress'd, I can find no rest, I will try the land
   of liberty.

My father holds five acres of land, it was not enough to
   support us all,
Which banishes me from my native land, to old Ireland
   dear I bid farewell.
My hardships here I can't endure, since here no longer I
   can stay
I take my lot and leave this spot and try the land of liberty.

My love, you know that trade is low, provisions they're
   exceeding high,
We see the poor from door to door craving their wants we
   can't supply,
To hear their moans, their sighs and groans, with children
   naked cold and bare,
Crave, say relief, it renews my grief as we have nothing for
   to spare.

So now my dear you need not fear the dangers of the raging
   sea,
If your mind is bent I am content, so now prepare and
   come away.
She says, "My dear if you'll agree to marry me, I'll quickly
   prepare,
We'll join our hands in wedlock's bands and we will stay
   no longer here."

It was in the year of '46 I was forced to leave my native
    land,
To old Ireland I bid adieu and to my fond relations all,
But now I'm in America, no rents or taxes we pay at all,
So now I bid a long farewell to my native and old
    Donegal.

George Zimmerman, ed., *Songs of Irish Rebellion* (Hatboro,
Pa.: Folklore Associates, 1967), pp. 236-37.

4.
Partition

The Great Famine was Ireland's holocaust. Just as the state of Israel emerged from the concentration camps, so the state of Ireland came from the famine. In the 1860s Isaac Butt founded the Home Rule party, which soon won most of the Irish seats in Parliament — except those in Ulster. Under Charles Stewart Parnell the party demanded the repeal of the Act of Union, as well as the grant of internal self-government to the whole of Ireland, and after a sustained campaign persuaded William Gladstone, the British Prime Minister, that its demands were just. Thus in 1886 Gladstone introduced into Parliament a bill granting Home Rule — and in doing so split his own party, the Liberals, and prompted a Protestant backlash, of which the Conservatives, led by Lord Randolph Churchill, took advantage, declaring that the bill was "a conspiracy against the honour of Britain and the welfare of Ireland."

Be that as it may, Ulster's Protestants knew that if Dublin got a parliament they would be dominated by the Catholic majority whom they had so long oppressed. As one of their slogans put it, "Home Rule means Rome Rule." To resist, they formed Orange Lodges (named after their hero William of Orange, victor of the Battle of the Boyne) and, in the name of religion, rioted in the streets of Belfast. One observer drily commented that "God does not expect such high zeal from his zealots." In 1891 Parnell was cited for adultery in a divorce. The scandal shocked Victorian morality, split the Irish party, and set back Home Rule for a generation.

Gladstone's Introduction to the First Home Rule Bill in the House of Commons (8 April 1886)

Since the last half-century dawned we have been steadily engaged in extending, as well as in consolidating, free institutions. I divide the period since the act of union with Ireland into two — the first from 1800 to 1832, the epoch of what is still justly called the great reform act; and secondly, from 1833 to 1885. I do not know whether it has been as widely observed as I think it deserves to be that, in the first of those periods — 32 years — there were no less than 11 years — it may seem not much to say, but wait for what is coming — there were no less than 11 of those 32 years in which our statute book was free throughout the whole year from repressive legislation of an exceptional kind against Ireland. But in the 53 years since we advanced far in the career of liberal principles and actions — in those 53 years, from 1833 to 1885 — there were but two years which were entirely free from the action of this special legislation for Ireland. Is not that of itself almost enough to prove we have arrived at the point where it is necessary that we should take a careful and searching survey of our position? . . .

Well, Sir, what are the results that have been produced? This result above all — and now I come to what I consider to be the basis of the whole mischief — that rightly or wrongly, yet in point of fact, law is discredited in Ireland, and discredited in Ireland upon this ground especially — that it comes to the people of that country with a foreign aspect, and in a foreign garb. . . .

England, by her own strength, and by her vast majority in this house, makes her own laws just as independently as if she were not combined with two other countries. Scotland — a small country, smaller than Ireland, but a country endowed with a spirit so masculine that never in the long course of history, excepting for two brief periods, each of a few years, was the superior strength of England such as to enable her to put down the national freedom beyond the border — Scotland, wisely recognized by England, has been allowed and encouraged in this house to make her own laws as freely and as effectually as if she had a representation six times as strong. The consequence is that the mainspring of law in England is felt by the people to be English; the mainspring of law in Scotland is felt by the people to be Scotch; but the mainspring of law in Ireland is not felt by the people to be Irish. . . .

I will deviate from my path for a moment to say a word upon the state of opinion in that wealthy, intelligent, and energetic portion of the Irish community which, as I have said, predominates in a certain portion of Ulster. Our duty is to adhere to sound general principles, and to give the utmost consideration we can to the opinions of that energetic minority. The first thing of all, I should say, is that if, upon any occasion, by any individual or section, violent measures have been threatened in certain emergencies, I think the best compliment I can pay to those who have threatened us is to take no notice whatever of the threats, but to treat them as momentary ebullitions, which will pass away with the fears from which they spring, and at the same time to adopt on our part every reasonable measure for disarming those fears. I cannot conceal the conviction that the voice of Ireland, as a whole, is at this moment clearly and constitutionally spoken. I cannot say it is otherwise when five-sixths of its lawfully-chosen representatives are of one mind in this matter. There is a counter voice; and I wish to know what is the claim of those by whom that counter voice is spoken, and how much is the scope and allowance we can give them. Certainly, Sir, I cannot allow it to be said that a protestant minority in Ulster, or elsewhere, is to rule the question at large for Ireland. I am aware of no constitutional doctrine tolerable on which such a conclusion could be adopted or justified. But I think that the protestant minority should have its wishes considered to the utmost practicable extent in any form which they may assume.

Various schemes, short of refusing the demand of Ireland at large, have been proposed on behalf of Ulster. One scheme is, that Ulster itself, or, perhaps with more appearance of reason, a portion of Ulster, should be excluded from the operation of the bill we are about to introduce. Another scheme is, that certain rights with regard to certain subjects — such, for example, as education and some other subjects — should be reserved and should be placed, to a certain extent, under the control of provincial councils. These, I think, are the suggestions which reached me in different shapes; there may be others. But what I wish to say of them is this — there is no one of them which has appeared to us to be so completely justified, either upon its merits or by the weight of opinion supporting and recommending it, as to warrant our including it in the bill and proposing it to parliament upon our responsibility. . . .

Parliamentary Debates, 3d ser., vol. 304, col. 1036-85, in E. Curtis and R. B. McDowell, eds., *Irish Historical Documents, 1172-1922* (London: Methuen, 1943), pp. 287-91.

British Government Report on the Belfast Riots (1886)

The Warrant in the first place charges us with the duty of inquiring into the origin and circumstances and the causes of the continuance of the riots and disturbances which disgraced Belfast, in the months of June, July, August and September, 1886, and which, up to the time of our holding the inquiry, had caused a loss of at least twenty-nine lives, and a destruction of property, direct and indirect, which one witness estimated at £90,000, but the exact amount of which is at present impossible to calculate.

Belfast is a great manufacturing town, which in progress and wealth enjoys a foremost place among the centres of population of the United Kingdom. Its population in 1881, according to the Census returns, was 208,122, and since that time has probably increased to about 230,000. It has an area of 6,805 acres, and a valuation of £604,537. The town is, in its present proportions, of very recent growth, and the result is that the poorer classes, instead of as in other countries, occupying tenements in large houses, reside mainly in separate cottages or small houses. The western district of Belfast is covered with these small dwellings of the artisan and labourer; and this district was the main theatre of the riots of 1886.

The extremity to which party and religious feeling has grown in Belfast is shown strikingly by the fact that the people of the artisan and labouring class, disregarding the ordinary considerations of convenience, dwell to a large extent in separate quarters, each of which is almost entirely given up to persons of one particular faith, and the boundaries of which are sharply defined. In the district of West Belfast, the great thoroughfare of Shankhill-road, with the network of streets running into it, and the side streets connecting those lateral branches, is an almost purely Protestant district; and the parties referred to in the evidence as "the Shankhill mob" are a Protestant mob. The great Catholic quarter is due south of the Shankhill district, and consists of the thoroughfare known as the Falls-road, and the streets running south of it; and the parties referred to in the testimony before us as "the Falls-road mob" are therefore a Catholic mob. Due south of the Falls district is Grosvenor-street; almost entirely inhabited by Protestants, so that the Catholic quarter lies between two Protestant districts. The Shankhill-road and Falls-road are both largely inhabited by shopkeepers who supply the wants of the population, and whose houses are sometimes large and comfortable. The streets running off these thoroughfares consist of long rows of cottages of artisans and labourers. The great points of danger to the peace of the town are open spaces in the border land between the two quarters; and two of those spaces — the Brickfields and Springfields — will be found to have been the theatres of some of the worst scenes of the riots.

The great number of working people who dwell in the districts we have described are, at ordinary times, a most peaceable and industrious community. But unfortunately a spirit has grown up among those people, which has resulted in that, on three previous occasions within the last thirty years, in 1857, 1864, and 1872, the town was the scene of disturbances and long-continued riots. . . .

The month of June, 1886, opened in Belfast upon a condition of great excitement and high party feeling. The Home Rule Bill was then before Parliament; and the measure evoked strong feeling in Belfast. The Catholics, as a body, supported the

Bill. The Protestants, as a body regarded it with hostility. The result was that this apparently political question evoked the spirit of sectarian animosity. A general election was regarded as inevitable; and in one of the Divisions of Belfast, parties were so evenly balanced, that a keen and close contest was certain. . . .

We now report to your Excellency that the origin of the riots and disturbances into which we have been directed to inquire may be traced to the unfortunate combination of the following circumstances: The strong political feeling generally prevailing in Belfast; the feverish excitement produced by the General Election in December, 1885, followed in January by the change of Ministry, together with the sudden and unexpected advance of the Home Rule question; The agitation for and against Home Rule, and the preparations for another General Election, which were carried on from January to July with great earnestness by both political parties; On the 3rd June, the Blakely and Murphy incident, trivial in itself, but a spark in the midst of combustible material; On the 4th June, the scandalous outrage committed by a section of the anti-Home Rule party on the Alexandra Dock labourers, causing the death of the young lad, Curran; On Sunday, 6th June, the demonstration and wanton rioting by a section of the Home Rule party, on the occasion of Curran's funeral; At the critical period prior to this, the want of effective preparation by any of the authorities in Belfast to anticipate these and like emergencies; the neglect to call together the borough magistracy, especially as the temporary absence of the Mayor only rendered the necessity for their meeting more imperative; On Monday, 7th June, the ill-advised display of a small force of both military and police at The Queen's Island yard; Lastly, the order issued on this date that a number of the police should carry their rifles and side arms when on duty in the streets of Belfast, an order which appears to have been contrary to the spirit, if not to the letter of the constabulary code, and which, in our opinion, whilst it certainly impaired the efficiency of the police force, may have tended greatly to increase the excitement and restless distrust already stirred up in the anti-Home Rule party. . . .

James Cary, ed., *Ireland, a Documentary History* (Dublin: Fallon, 1949–51), II, pp. 126–28.

During the constitutional crisis of 1910 the Liberal government needed the votes of Irish Members of Parliament to curb the powers of the House of Lords, and in return it agreed to grant Home Rule, to take effect in 1914. The reaction of Ulster's Unionists was even more intense than it had been in 1886. Spurred by the opposition Conservative party — whose leader, Bonar Law, had declared that "Ulster will fight and Ulster will be right" — Unionists prepared to defy the law. "Don't be afraid of illegalities," exhorted the foremost Unionist, Edward Carson, a distinguished lawyer who went on to become Attorney General.

In 1912, 471,000 Unionists — well over half of Ulster's Protestant population — signed (some with their own blood) a solemn league and covenant defying the authority of Parliament. More ominous, they started to import guns, prompting Padraic Pearse, the Catholic poet and Nationalist leader, to remark: "The Orangeman with the rifle is a much less ridiculous figure than the nationalist without a rifle." So the South, too, armed, and by the summer of 1914 civil war seemed imminent.

BRITISH INTELLIGENCE REPORTS ON THE STATE OF IRELAND (1912-1914)

Political feeling ran high in Ulster during the year 1912. The first display of this feeling occurred in connection with the visit of the First Lord of the Admiralty (the Right Hon. Winston Churchill, M.P.) to Belfast on the 8th February, 1912, to address a meeting in favour of Home Rule, when the Unionist Council refused to allow the Ulster Hall to be used, and the meeting had to be held in a huge tent erected in the Celtic Park Club's Football Ground, situated in a Nationalist quarter of the City.

The Unionist Club movement made great progress during the earlier months of the year, and drilling was extensively carried on by members of these Clubs and Orange Lodges, the immediate object in view being to present a disciplined appearance at the Unionist Demonstration at Balmoral Show Grounds, Belfast, on

Easter Tuesday, 9th April, to protest against Home Rule. About 300,000 persons, it is computed, attended this demonstration, at which the principal speakers were Mr. Bonar Law, M.P., and Sir Edward Carson, M.P. The effect of the military training was very noticeable as the Club contingents marched in procession through the streets of Belfast to the place of meeting.

Another move in the campaign in Ulster was the holding of a series of demonstrations throughout the Province, all leading up to the signing, on "Ulster Day," Saturday, the 28th September, 1912, of a solemn covenant to resist Home Rule, of which the following is a copy:—

ULSTER'S SOLEMN LEAGUE AND COVENANT

Being convinced in our consciences that Home Rule would be disastrous, to the material well-being of Ulster as well as the whole of Ireland, subversive of our civil and religious freedom, destructive of our citizenship, and perilous to the unity of the Empire, we, whose names are underwritten, men of Ulster, loyal subjects of His Gracious Majesty King George V., humbly relying on the God Whom our fathers in days of stress and trial confidently trusted, do hereby pledge ourselves in solemn Covenant throughout this our time of threatened calamity to stand by one another in defending for ourselves and our children our cherished position of equal citizenship in the United Kingdom, and in using all means which may be found necessary to defeat the present conspiracy to set up a Home Rule Parliament in Ireland.

And in the event of such a Parliament being forced upon us, we further solemnly and mutually pledge ourselves to refuse to recognize its authority.

In sure confidence that God will defend the right we hereto subscribe our names.

And, further, we individually declare that we have not already signed this Covenant.

The above was signed by me at _____ "Ulster Day," Saturday, 28th September, 1912.

GOD SAVE THE KING . . .

In March, 1913, information was received by the Police that ten cases of discarded Italian Army rifles reached West Hartlepool from Hamburg via Newcastle-on-Tyne and that it was intended to forward these cases to Belfast. The cases were duly forwarded, but were secretly put ashore at Newcastle on the 27th March, where they remained until the middle of June, when they were forwarded by different routes to prominent leaders of the Unionist Party in Ulster, viz., Lord Leitrim, Captain Waring, and Messrs. Combe, Archdale, and Liddle. These arms were, on arrival, seized by the Customs Authorities.

Towards the end of May, 1913, information was received by the Police that a very large quantity of arms had been received from abroad and were being re-packed at the Windsor Castle Hotel, Hammersmith, for conveyance to Ireland. The London Metropolitan Police kept the matter under closest observation, with the result that a consignment of 600 rifles and bayonets to Belfast, for Messrs. Herdman & Co., Strabane, described as "Electrical plant"; and a consignment of 300 rifles and bayonets to Dublin in a furniture van, for Lord Farnham, Cavan (all being discarded Italian Army rifles), were detained and seized by the Customs Authorities on the ground of misdescription within the meaning of the Customs Laws. In all, 1,166 rifles and bayonets were seized by the Customs Authorities at Dublin, Belfast, Coleraine, Londonderry, Greenore, and Drogheda, and, in accordance with the decision of His Majesty's Government, all these arms were handed over to the Military Authorities for destruction on the expiration of a period of six months from the date of seizures unless, in the meantime, any claims to them are put forward by the persons to whom they were consigned.

The Police have information that, in the month of June, 1912, two consignments of foreign rifles reached West Hartlepool from abroad, and that although they have been unable to trace the conveyance of these arms to Ireland there can be no doubt that they reached this country. . . .

On the occasion of the celebration of the "Opening of the Gates of Derry" on the 12th August, 1913, about 9,000 persons arrived in the City by special trains from Belfast and the Counties of Antrim, Armagh, Down and Tyrone. The conduct of some of these persons when proceeding to Derry by train was very bad, as they kept up a continuous fusillade of revolver shots from the railway carriages in which they were travelling. After Divine

Service in the Cathedral the procession, which had originally started from the Wall, reformed and proceeded at 1.45 p.m. over the usual route, which included the principal streets of the City. At Waterloo Street a Nationalist crowd collected and attempted to attack the procession when passing. The police, however, drove this crowd back, but when the procession was returning some stones were thrown by the Nationalists and a few bottles by the processionists, who also fired several revolver shots. The police dispersed the Nationalists and forced the processionists on, and in this way prevented any further disturbance along the route of the procession.

When the Rosemount Band was going home about 4.15 p.m. on the same date stones were thrown at it by Nationalists at Waterloo Street and other points. The police dispersed the stone-throwers at every point. The crowd accompanying the band also threw some stones and fired several revolver shots.

In the evening when the Orangemen were marching towards the railway stations revolver-firing was quite general, and at the Great Northern Railway it was almost continuous. There was great excitement outside the station for a couple of hours — from 5 to 7 p.m. — and there were some isolated assaults on individuals belonging to both parties. A strong force of police was present and prevented any serious disturbance. While endeavouring to save a man who was being attacked by Nationalists the Mayor of Derry was struck on the back of the head with a stone and slightly injured. . . .

At midnight on 1st August, 1914, a police patrol at Kilcool Railway Station saw a sailing boat or smack arrive off Kilcool and lower her sails when about 200 yards from the shore. Immediately afterwards a motor boat arrived and went alongside the smack. On observing this the police patrol made a move to leave the station and get down to the shore when they were prevented doing so by a body of men who had been in ambush close to the station. Then a green char-a-banc of Thompson's, Dublin, accompanied by two motor cars, arrived at the station and the work of landing the arms commenced. In all about 100 bales of rifles packed in canvas and straw and about 100 cases of ammunition in boxes were landed. They were placed in the char-a-banc and motor cars, and some were served out to the men employed as guards. As far as the police could judge about 250 men were present. All their conversation was in Irish. The men assembled on bicycles and left the same way. The work was finished about 2 a.m. (2nd August), but the police patrol was not allowed to leave until forty minutes later. At 5 a.m. a green char-a-banc passed through Bray to Dublin, and half an hour later a red motor lorry laden with men, while cyclists in some numbers also passed through up to 6 a.m., all going fast towards Dublin. The men engaged in the work were all strangers to the police patrol at Kilcool, and none of the cyclists seen at Bray were known to the police there. The police believed the work was done by some Dublin Corps of Volunteers. Other motor cars must have been waiting to take some of the party back, but the police patrol could not see them, the night being dark and misty. The men engaged in the gun-running had long batons and revolvers, and a large number of scouts were out in addition to the 250 men on the shore.

On the journey to Dublin it appears that the char-a-banc broke down and the guns were then transferred to the other motor cars engaged in the work. The police were informed that between 1 and 2 p.m. on Sunday, 2nd August, at least eight motor cars laden with arms pulled up outside 206 Great Brunswick Street, the Headquarters of the National Volunteers, which the drivers entered and left shortly afterwards, driving their cars away in different directions. No guns or military equipment were taken into the premises.

Breandan MacGiolla Choille, ed., *Chief Secretary's Office, Dublin, Intelligence Notes Preserved in the State Paper Office* (Dublin: Rialtas na h-Eireann, 1966), pp. 6–7, 18–19, 21, 114.

Even though in 1914 hundreds of thousands of Irishmen of both faiths flocked to volunteer for the British army, the outbreak of the First World War did not prevent a civil war in Ireland. It merely postponed one, making the eventual climax even bloodier. On Easter Monday 1916 the Nationalists seized the public buildings in Dublin, proclaiming the birth of an Irish Republic. Although the British army quickly crushed the rising by shooting the rebel leaders, this so alienated Irish public opinion that by 1918 England had lost control of the South. Only the Protestants of the North remained loyal to the crown, utterly refusing to accept rule from Dublin. So in 1920 the British, while making vague promises about a council for all of Ireland, partitioned Ireland.

Meanwhile the war between the Nationalists and the British, which had erupted into open fighting in 1919, dragged on until late 1921, when the former, exhausted by war, and the latter, disgusted with the excesses of their troops, especially the "Black and Tans," signed a treaty granting the twenty-six Southern counties independence within the British Empire, and recognizing the partition of Ireland.

The treaty brought Ireland nearly half a century of peace. It also sowed the seeds of the present crisis, which after so long a germination can hardly be expected to wither away.

THE PROCLAMATION OF THE IRISH REPUBLIC (1916)

Poblacht na h-Eireann
The Provisional Government
of the
IRISH REPUBLIC
To the people of Ireland

IRISHMEN AND IRISHWOMEN: In the name of God and of the dead generations from which she receives her old tradition of nationhood, Ireland, through us, summons her children to her flag and strikes for her freedom.

Having organised and trained her manhood through her secret revolutionary organisation, the Irish Republican Brotherhood, and through her open military organisations, the Irish Volunteers and the Irish Citizen Army, having patiently perfected her discipline, having resolutely waited for the right moment to reveal itself, she now seizes that moment and, supported by her exiled children in America and by gallant allies in Europe, but relying in the first on her own strength, she strikes in full confidence of victory.

We declare the right of the people of Ireland to the ownership of Ireland and to the unfettered control of Irish destinies to be sovereign and indefeasible. The long usurpation of that right by a foreign people and government has not extinguished the right, nor can it ever be extinguished except by the destruction of the Irish people. In every generation the Irish people have asserted their right to national freedom and sovereignty: six times during the past three hundred years they have asserted it in arms. Standing on that fundamental right and again asserting it in arms in the face of the world, we hereby proclaim the Irish Republic as a Sovereign Independent State, and we pledge our lives and the lives of our comrades-in-arms to the cause of its freedom, of its welfare and of its exaltation among the nations.

The Irish Republic is entitled to, and hereby claims, the allegiance of every Irishman and Irishwoman. The Republic guarantees religious and civil liberty, equal rights and equal opportunities to all its citizens, and declares its resolve to pursue the happiness and prosperity of the whole nation and of all its parts, cherishing all the children of the nation equally, and oblivious of the differences, carefully fostered by an alien government, which have divided a minority from the majority in the past.

Until our arms have brought the opportune moment for the establishing of a permanent National Government, representative of the whole people of Ireland, and elected by the suffrages of all her men and women, the Provisional Government, hereby constituted, will administer the civil and military affairs of the Republic in trust for the people. We place the cause of the Irish Republic under the protection of the Most High God, Whose blessing we invoke upon our arms, and we pray that no one who serves that cause will dishonour it by cowardice, inhumanity or rapine. In this supreme hour the Irish nation must, by its valour and discipline, and by the readiness of its children to sacrifice themselves for the common good, prove itself worthy of the august destiny to which it is called.

Signed on Behalf of the Provisional Government,

THOMAS J. CLARKE

SEAN MacDIARMADA   THOMAS MacDONAGH

P. H. PEARSE   EAMONN CEANNT

JAMES CONNOLLY   JOSEPH PLUNKETT

Tim Pat Coogan, *The I.R.A.* (London: Fontana, 1971), pp. 36–37.

THE PARTITION OF IRELAND (1920)

An act to provide for the better government of Ireland
Be it enacted . . .

1. (1) On and after the appointed day[1] there shall be established for Southern Ireland a parliament to be called the parliament of Southern Ireland consisting of his majesty, the senate of Southern Ireland, and the house of commons of Southern Ireland, and there shall be established for Northern Ireland a parliament to be called the parliament of Northern Ireland consisting of his majesty, the senate of Northern Ireland, and the house of commons of Northern Ireland.

(2) For the purposes of this act, Northern Ireland shall consist of the parliamentary counties of Antrim, Armagh, Down, Fermanagh, Londonderry, and Tyrone, and the parliamentary boroughs of Belfast and Londonderry, and Southern Ireland shall consist of so much of Ireland as is not comprised within the said parliamentary counties and boroughs.

2. (1) With a view to the eventual establishment of a parliament for the whole of Ireland, and to bringing about harmonious action between the parliaments and governments of Southern Ireland and Northern Ireland, and to the promotion of mutual intercourse and uniformity in relation to matters affecting the whole of Ireland, and to providing for the administration of services which the two parliaments mutually agree should be administered uniformly throughout the whole of Ireland, or which by virtue of this act are to be so administered, there shall be constituted, as soon as may be after the appointed day, a council to be called the council of Ireland.

(2) Subject as hereinafter provided, the council of Ireland shall consist of a person nominated by the lord lieutenant acting in accordance with instructions from his majesty who shall be president, and forty other persons, of whom seven shall be

---

[1] A date not later than fifteen months after the passing of the act, to be fixed by order of the British privy council.

members of the senate of Southern Ireland, thirteen shall be members of the house of commons of Southern Ireland, seven shall be members of the senate of Northern Ireland, and thirteen shall be members of the house of commons of Northern Ireland.

E. Curtis and R. B. McDowell, eds., *Irish Historical Documents, 1172-1922* (London: Methuen, 1943), pp. 297-98.

II
The
Current
Crisis

BELFAST: showing Sectarian areas

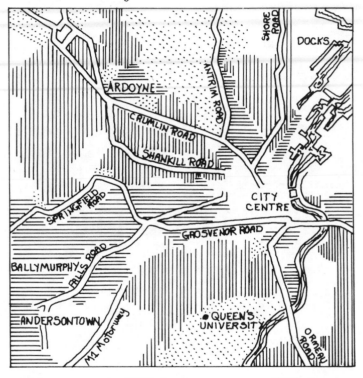

1.
The Crossroads

Even though Ireland has remained fairly peaceful in the half century after partition, the treaty of 1922 did not solve the Irish problem. Long-standing hatreds and injustices remained — and festered — as the two parts of Ireland drifted further and further apart.

In the South, disagreement over the 1922 treaty, which kept the Irish Free State in the British Empire and required its officials to swear allegiance to the King, resulted in a civil war that, after a year of bitter fighting, the pro-treaty forces won. The Irish Free State (which changed its name to Eire in 1937 and to the Republic of Ireland in 1947) became an increasingly Catholic and Celtic nation. Gaelic was, and is, an official language, required in schools and for civil service employment. The 1937 constitution declared that Eire was the legitimate government of the whole of Ireland, and recognized "the special position" of the Catholic church. The bishops have exercised considerable social and political influence, controlling primary and secondary education. Also, they have helped to defeat proposals for a national health scheme and to pass laws censoring literature and prohibiting divorce, abortion, and contraception.

The 1922 treaty did not improve relations between Britain and the South. In the 1930s the two countries engaged in a tariff war. During the Second World War, Irish neutrality and the loss of British naval bases on the west coast of Ireland added to Allied casualties in the Battle of the Atlantic. In April 1945 Eire was one of the few governments that expressed official condolences to the German ambassador on the death of Hitler.

As the South became more Catholic and Celtic, the North became a single-party Protestant enclave. As Lord Craigavon, Ulster's first Prime Minister, told the Stormont, its legislature, "All I boast is that we are a Protestant parliament and a Protestant people." The Unionists, the Protestant party, took advantage of their built-in majority to dominate Ulster's one-third Catholic minority, using the Stormont to pass such draconian laws as the 1922 Special Powers Act. Protestants got the best jobs in the post office, civil service, local government, and shipyards, and the Unionist party appointed only two high court judges who were not prominent Unionists.

The party also controlled the governments in areas where Catholics were a majority by barring tenants and lodgers (usually Catholics) from voting in local elections and by allowing owners of business property (invariably Protestants) as many as six votes. As if that were not enough, it resorted to gerrymandering, the most blatant example of which was Londonderry, where in the 1967 election 18,429 Catholics elected eight members of the city council — whereas twelve were elected by 8,721 Protestants.

Northern Ireland was, de facto, a segregated society. Protestants and Catholics lived in different parts of town; the former attended public, the latter parochial schools. The two did not even meet on the sports field; Catholics tended to play Gaelic football, Protestants soccer. There were few mixed marriages, and usually such couples found it wisest to leave Northern Ireland.

During the 1960s significant changes started. Pope. John's ecumenicalism made the church in the South more flexible. More important, in 1963 Terence O'Neill became Prime Minister of Northern Ireland and within five years created 22,000 new jobs and raised real income by 46 percent. This new prosperity encouraged the growth of a Catholic middle class that, through the Civil Rights Association, protested against discrimination. On 5 October 1968 in Londonderry, the police brutally broke up one of their marches in full view of the world's television cameras, and public reaction — frqm Britain especially — forced O'Neill to grant reforms. He ended multiple voting, the unfair system of allocating public housing, replaced the gerrymandered city council of Londonderry with a commission, and promised that city to create 12,000 new jobs and build 9,600 new houses by 1981.

But for many Catholics a dozen years was too long a wait, while for even more Protestants, whose watchword — like Dixie's — was "Never!" any appeasement was precipitate. So on December 9 the Prime Minister went on television to warn the people of Ulster that they stood at a crossroads. He sought the middle ground, but found a rapidly widening crevasse.

On the left, the leaders of the Civil Rights Association thought his speech "hilarious" and continued their program of marches, including one from Belfast to Londonderry in January 1969, which — as the police stood looking on — a Protestant mob attacked at Burntollet Bridge. On the right, support for O'Neill, already badly weakened by his efforts to improve relations with the South, further eroded in the election of February 1970 when Ian Paisley, the hard-line Protestant minister, nearly defeated the Prime Minister in his own constituency. Two months later O'Neill was forced to resign.

In late 1968 Ulster indeed stood at a crossroads; and it took the wrong turning.

THE SPECIAL POWERS ACT (1922)

An Act to empower certain authorities of the Government of Northern Ireland to take steps for preserving the peace and maintaining order in Northern Ireland, and for purposes connected therewith.

Be it enacted by the King's most Excellent Majesty, and the Senate and the House of Commons of Northern Ireland in this present Parliament assembled, and by the authority of the same, as follows:—

1.—(1) The civil authority shall have power, in respect of persons, matters and things within the jurisdiction of the Government of Northern Ireland, to take all such steps and issue all such orders as may be necessary for preserving the peace and maintaining order, according to and in the execution of this Act and the regulations contained in the Schedule thereto, or such regulations as may be made in accordance with the provisions of this Act (which regulations, whether contained in the said Schedule or made as aforesaid, are in this Act referred to as "the regulations"):

Provided that the ordinary course of law and avocations of life and the enjoyment of property shall be interfered with as little as may be permitted by the exigencies of the steps required to be taken under this Act.

(2) For the purposes of this Act the civil authority shall be the Minister of Home Affairs for Northern Ireland, but that Minister may delegate, either unconditionally or subject to such conditions as he thinks fit. . . .

4. A person convicted of an offence against the regulations shall be liable to be sentenced to imprisonment with or without hard labour for a term not exceeding two years or to a fine not exceeding one hundred pounds or to both· such imprisonment and fine, and the court may, in addition to any other sentence which may be imposed, order that any goods or articles in respect of which the offence has been committed shall be forfeited.

5. Where after trial by any court a person is convicted of any crime or offence to which this section applies, the court may, in addition to any other punishment which may lawfully be imposed, order such person, if a male, to be once privately whipped, and the provisions of subsection (6) of section thirty-seven of the Larceny Act, 1916, as to sentences of whipping shall apply accordingly.

6. A crime under section two or section three of the Explosive Substances Act, 1883, shall be a crime punishable by death: provided that this section shall not apply to any such crime committed before the passing of this Act.

Where a sentence of death is pronounced by the court upon conviction for a crime to which this section applies, the sentence may be pronounced and carried into execution, and all other proceedings thereupon and in respect thereof may be had and taken, in the same manner as sentence might have been pronounced and carried into execution, and proceedings might have been had and taken, upon a conviction for murder. . . .

10.—(1) For the purpose of preserving the peace and maintaining order, the Minister of Home Affairs may
        (a) Prohibit the holding of inquests by coroners on dead bodies in any area in Northern Ireland. . . .

Northern Ireland, The Public General Acts of 1922 (Belfast: H.M.S.O., no date), pp. 6–12.

"Ulster Stands at the Crossroads": Prime Minister O'Neill's Television Address (9 December 1968)

Ulster stands at the crossroads. I believe you know me well enough by now to appreciate that I am not a man given to extravagant language. But I must say to you this evening that our conduct over the coming days and weeks will decide our future. And as we face this situation, I would be failing in my duty to you as your Prime Minister if I did not put the issues, calmly and clearly before you all. These issues are far too serious to be determined behind closed doors, or left to noisy minorities. The time has come for the people as a whole to speak in a clear voice.

For more than five years now I have tried to heal some of the deep divisions in our community. I did so because I could not see how an Ulster divided against itself could hope to stand. I made it clear that a Northern Ireland based upon the interests of any one section rather than upon the interests of all could have no long-term future. . . .

In Londonderry and other places recently, a minority of agitators determined to subvert lawful authority played a part in setting light to highly inflammable material. But the tinder for that fire, in the form of grievances real or imaginary, had been piling up for years.

And so I saw it as our duty to do two things. First, to be firm in the maintenance of law and order, and in resisting those elements which seek to profit from any disturbances. Secondly, to ally firmness with fairness, and to look at any underlying causes of dissension which were troubling decent and moderate people. As I saw it, if we were not prepared to face up to our problems, we would have to meet mounting pressure both internally, from those who were seeking change, and externally from British public and parliamentary opinion, which had been deeply disturbed by the events in Londonderry.

That is why it has been my view from the beginning that we should decide — of our own free will and as a responsible Government in command of events — to press on with a continuing programme of change to secure a united and harmonious community. This, indeed, has been my aim for over five years.

Moreover, I knew full well that Britain's financial and other support for Ulster, so laboriously built up, could no longer be guaranteed if we failed to press on with such a programme. . . . Because Westminster has trusted us over the years to use the powers of Stormont for the good of all the people of Ulster, a sound custom has grown up that Westminster does not use its supreme authority in fields where we are normally responsible. But Mr. Wilson [the British Prime Minister] made it absolutely clear to us that if we did not face up to our problems the Westminster Parliament might well decide to act over our heads. Where would our Constitution be then? What shred of self-respect would be left to us? If we allowed others to solve our problems because we had not the guts — let me use a plain word — the guts to face up to them, we would be utterly shamed.

There are, I know, today some so-called loyalists who talk of independence from Britain — who seem to want a kind of Protestant Sinn Fein [the political wing of the IRA]. These people will not listen when they are told that Ulster's income is £200 million a year but that we can spend £300 million — only because Britain pays the balance.

Rhodesia, in defying Britain from thousands of miles away, at least has an Air Force and an Army of her own. Where are the Ulster armoured divisions or the Ulster jet planes? They do not exist and we could not afford to buy them. These people are not merely extremists. They are lunatics who would set a course along a road which could only lead at the end into an all-Ireland Republic. They are not loyalists but *dis*loyalists: disloyal to Britain, disloyal to the Constitution, disloyal to the Crown, disloyal — if they are in public life — to the solemn oaths they have sworn to Her Majesty the Queen.

But these considerations, important though they are, are not my main concern. What I seek — and I ask for the help and understanding of you all — is a swift end to the growing civil disorder throughout Ulster. For as matters stand today, we are on the brink of chaos, where neighbour could be set against neighbour. It is simple-minded to imagine that problems such as these can be solved by repression. I for one am not willing to expose our police force to indefinite insult and injury. Nor am I prepared to see the shopkeepers and traders of Ulster wrecked and looted for the benefit of the rabble. We must tackle root causes if this agitation is to be contained. We must be able to say to the moderate on both sides: come with us into a new era of cooperation, and leave the extremists to the law. But this I also say to all, Protestant or Roman Catholic, Unionist or Nationalist: disorder must now cease. We are taking the necessary measures to strengthen our police forces. Determined as we are to act with absolute fairness, we will also be resolute in restoring respect for the laws of the land. . . .

And now I want to say a word directly to those who have been demonstrating for Civil Rights. The changes which we have announced are genuine and far-reaching changes and the Government as a whole is totally committed to them. I would not continue to preside over an Administration which would water them down or make them meaningless. You will see when the members of the Londonderry Commission are appointed that we intend to live up to our words that this will be a body to command confidence and respect. You will see that in housing allocations we mean business. You will see that legislation to appoint an Ombudsman will be swiftly introduced. Perhaps you are not entirely satisfied; but this is a democracy, and I ask you now with all sincerity to call your people off the streets and allow an atmosphere favourable to change to develop. You are Ulstermen yourselves. You know we are all of us stubborn people, who will not be pushed too far. I believe that most of you want change, not revolution. Your voice has been heard, and clearly heard. Your duty now is to play your part in taking the heat out of the situation before blood is shed. . . .

And now a further word to you all. What kind of Ulster do you want? A happy and respected Province, in good standing with the rest of the United Kingdom? Or a place continually torn apart by riots and demonstrations, and regarded by the rest of Britain as a political outcast? As always in a democracy, the choice is yours. I will accept whatever your verdict may be. If it is your decision that we should live up to the words "Ulster is British" which is part of our creed, then my services will be at your disposal to do what I can. But if you should want a separate, inward-looking, selfish and divided Ulster then you must seek for others to lead you along that road, for I cannot and will not do it. Please weigh well all that is at stake, and make your voice heard in whatever way you think best, so that we may know the views *not* of the few *but* of the many. For this is truly a time of decision, and in your silence *all* that we have built up could be lost. I pray that you will reflect carefully and decide wisely. And I ask all our Christian people, whatever their denomination, to attend their places of worship on Sunday next to pray for the peace and harmony of our country.

Terence O'Neill, *Ulster at the Crossroads* (London: Faber and Faber, 1969), pp. 140–46.

2.
Unionist Views

There is a story of the journalist who asked an Ulsterman if he went to church. "I'm an atheist," the latter replied, "but, by God, I'm a Protestant atheist!" In Northern Ireland religion is a matter not just of the way one worships one's maker but of how one votes. Protestants invariably support the Unionist party, Catholics one of the Nationalist groups. When in the early 1950s a visting English Jesuit asked some friends in Derry if they knew of any exceptions to this rule, they paused before replying that they thought a Protestant professor at a local college was really a Nationalist though he professed to be a Communist, thinking it safer that way.

Religion in Northern Ireland — as in Israel — tends to determine one's loyalty, or disloyalty, to the state. Many Ulstermen — like many Israelis — feel threatened by external enemies and internal subversives, and fear that one day their protectors, Britain or the United States, may sell them out. As one Protestant pamphleteer recently put it, "Ulster, like modern Israel, can only lose once."

Just as Israel has Masada, Ulster has Londonderry, and both countries share something of a fortress mentality. In Ulster this would help explain Protestants' discrimination against Catholics. Why should a state — hard-line Protestants would argue — grant full political rights to people who refuse to accept the legitimacy of that state? After all, the United States makes aliens swear that they do not intend to overthrow the government before it allows them to settle or take up citizenship.

But many of Ulster's Protestants are not interested in assimilating alien or, perhaps, modern ideas. As Ian Paisley's letter suggests, they are steeped in the conflicts of the past and want to maintain Ulster as an exclusively Protestant state. Indeed, Paisley petitions the second Queen Elizabeth as if he were living in the reign of the first. In his pamphlet *Ulster Must Fight,* Clifford Smyth sees the province's Protestants almost as the Chosen People of the Old Testament, while the recruiting pamphlet for the Ulster Volunteer Force, a Protestant private army, gives the impression that it is all too ready to help the Almighty help his people. Even moderate Protestants, such as Bill Henderson, seem preoccupied with the specter of an IRA-led Catholic conspiracy.

REV. IAN PAISLEY'S LETTER TO QUEEN ELIZABETH (MAY 1969)

YOUR GRACIOUS MAJESTY,

On behalf of many thousands of your most loyal subjects, we address this petition to you.

These subjects have requested us to assure you that they pray continually to Almighty God that you may be given grace and wisdom to govern all your subjects in the way that shall bring both upon you and them the benediction and blessing of Heaven.

Your visit to this particular General Assembly, when a representative to the Church of Rome is for the first time being received, gravely alarms those for whom we have the honour and authority to speak. We would respectfully remind Your Majesty that the last occasion on which you visited the Assembly was to commemorate the glorious Reformation of the 16th century. We submit that all that glorious event accomplished for the Scottish Kirk is now jeopardized by this intention to make you a party to the welcoming of a representative of that Church from whose fetters John Knox was raised up by God to deliver us. We condemn the action of the Assembly's hierarchy in using Your

Gracious Person and Royal Authority to accomplish their false
ecumenical ends. These actions we most solemnly protest. They
are neither in keeping with Bible Christianity nor with the laws
of your realm. Further, they ignore the whole basis and spirit of
the Coronation ceremony and the safeguards of the Bill of Rights.

We humbly request that Your Majesty will make it
abundantly clear that you will not consent to any deviation from
or violation of your Coronation oath, but will ever maintain the
Protestant Religion.

John Knox said that he feared one Mass in Scotland more
than a regiment of the enemy. Your subjects fear the result of the
proposed welcome to this idolatrous Mass-mongering representative of the Papal Antichrist and look to you to fulfil for them the
words of the prophecy of Isaiah concerning the Church in
Chapter 49, Verse 23 — "And kings shall be thy nursing fathers,
and their queens thy nursing mothers."

Protestant Telegraph, 31 May 1969.

"ULSTER MUST FIGHT" (1972)

With Faith in the God of their fathers, even with their bare
hands, Ulster-men are a match for the perpetrators of this cruel
and well programmed conspiracy. It is the Old Testament
partnership — "the Sword of the Lord and of Gideon." The
divisions in the ranks can be traced in the main to rivalries and
jealousies rather than to deep political cleavages, though there is
a distinction between the evangelical fervour of Dr. Paisley's
U.D.U.P. and the more materialistic and small "p" Protestant
position of some of the other loyalist groupings.

The Protestant pitch is also queered by the underground
communist element which ought not to be discounted, and by the
existence of some of the gangs of youths who have fallen a prey to
devious and unthinking leadership that has detracted from the
loyalist cause rather than added to it.

Let there be no mistaking the Protestant intention to stand

and fight for Ulster. The IRA Republican elements are making great sacrifices, while the Protestant population have steadfastly endured as the targets of the terror tactics of the Roman Catholic Nationalists. When the moment of truth comes, Ulster will fight and the weak things of this world will yet confound the mighty.

> Are you arming brother Protestants? Are you arming for the fray?
> Have you resolved on victory, and crushing Papal sway?
> And do you dare in solemn trust upon the King of Kings,
> To fight your battles underneath the shadow of His wings?
> Have you thought, ye patient Protestants, how you have been betrayed?
> By rulers who, of all your truth, a jest and mockery made?
> And think you, tis for them you arm, for them you strive and fight?
> No, No, — but for your own loved houses, in which your hearts' delight.

Clifford Smyth, *Ulster Must Fight* (Belfast: Puritan Printing Co., 1972), p. 4.

Ulster Volunteer Force Recruiting Circular (1971)

BEING CONVINCED that the enemies of our Faith and Freedom are determined to destroy the State of Northern Ireland and thereby enslave the people of God, we call on all members of our Loyalist Institutions, and other responsible citizens, to organise themselves IMMEDIATELY into Platoons of twenty under the command of someone capable of acting as Sergeant. Every effort must be made to arm these Platoons with whatever weapons are available. The first duty of each platoon will be to formulate a plan for the defence of its own street or road in co-operation with platoons in adjoining areas. A structure of command is already in existence and the various platoons will eventually be linked in a co-ordinated effort.

INSTRUCTIONS

Under no circumstances must Platoons come into open conflict with Her Majesty's Forces or the Police. If through wrong political direction Her Majesty's Forces are directed against loyalist people, members of Platoons must do everything possible to prevent a confrontation. WE ARE LOYALISTS, WE ARE QUEEN'S MEN. Our enemies are the forces of Romanism and Communism, which must be destroyed.

Members of platoons must act with the highest sense of responsibility and urgency in preparing our people for the full assault of the enemies within our Provinces and the forces of the Eire Government which will eventually be thrown against us. We must prepare for this! This Total War!

Members of platoons must work unceasingly to restore normality within our Protestant districts. Every effort must be made to clean up and repair damaged property and get the business life of the community flowing again. In this way we can prevent the enemy destroying the economic well being of our people.

Vandalism, destruction of property and looting must be dealt with without mercy.

Interventions by United Nations Forces or Direct Rule from Westminster MUST BE RESISTED. If such is proposed further instructions will be issued. The future of Northern Ireland will be determined by the courage, the heroism and the sacrifice of Ulster Protestants. No one must be allowed to interfere with that sacred trust.

STORMONT MUST RULE   GOD SAVE THE QUEEN

Danny Kennally and Eric Peterson, *Belfast, August 1971: A Case to be answered* (London: Independent Labour Party, 1971), pp. 14–15.

STATEMENT BY MR. BILL HENDERSON, CHAIRMAN OF ULSTER UNIONIST PARTY'S PUBLICITY COMMITTEE (1972)

Mr. Chairman, my family have lived in Northern Ireland since the early 1800's and have been connected with publishing for six generations. We publish a near 100,000 daily paper, the *Belfast Newsletter*, Monday through Saturday and a Sunday paper, the *Sunday News*, selling nearly 125,000 copies. We do not as a publishing concern permit religious discrimination and employ Protestants and Roman Catholics at all levels, including high executive office. The assistant editor of the *Newsletter* is a Roman Catholic and both the editor and the deputy editor of the *Sunday News* are Roman Catholics.

I served in the Irish Guards during the 1939–45 war and was proud to be in a regiment 50–50 Protestant and Roman Catholic and never saw any religious or political bickering or friction. The Irish Guards were and still are recruited about one-third each from Northern Ireland, the Republic of Ireland and Great Britain. It is significant that citizens of Eire joined with us and the United States in the war against Fascism and Nazism. However, the Government of the Republic of Ireland preserved a strict neutrality even to the extent of denying the use of Irish ports from which Allied naval forces could have set forth to save some of the ships and crews which were sunk by the Nazi U-boats in the Atlantic.

Never during those years of trial and testing for freedom and democracy did the Southern Irish Government offer any support, and indeed we should recall the Irish rebellion of 1916 when Britain was stabbed in the back when once again the free world was threatened by tyrannical forces. History certainly repeats itself.

I was for 5 years a Member in the Parliament of Northern Ireland, and presently hold senior office in the Unionist Party. This party has regularly been returned at successive free, fully enfranchised and democratic elections to provide the government of the province of Ulster.

Since 1921 the Eire Government has constantly maintained a policy of annexation toward Northern Ireland, notwithstanding the strong and continuing support for the British connection shown by the majority will of Northern Irish voters.

Is it surprising that the majority community in Ulster, regardless of class, religion or other affiliations, feel fearful of our southern neighbors with their nationalistic and covetous eyes continually on our fair and prosperous land and industry?

As a community the Ulster people, or the Scotch-Irish as we are often called, have close connections with the United States. Some 11 Presidents of the United States came from Ulster and Thomas Jefferson, one of our sons, wrote your Declaration of Independence. Indeed, a Mr. Dunlap from Strabane in County Tyrone actually printed the Declaration.

The past 3 years of violence in Ulster has certainly enjoyed worldwide publicity and we would claim that many activists and protagonists from all quarters have received a patronage, often highly rewarding in cash terms, from the media of the world that in my opinion has exacerbated a highly intractable problem.

What few realize is that the blueprint for the past 3 years of violence was written as long ago as 1966 and I now table a photostat from my own newspaper, the *Belfast Newsletter,* of May 21, 1966. This shows some alarming plans. I now quote some short extracts.

The IRA document captured in Eire includes a lengthy plan to take over Northern Ireland with the aid of an "armed stand" in the heart of Belfast, and an appeal to the United Nations, it was disclosed in Dublin last night.

What is so frightening about the document? From reliable sources I learn that it contains not only details of plans for an eventual military takeover by the IRA in the North, but also plans to prepare for this by infiltrating the British Army and Navy, the RUC and "B" Specials.

The document also contains plans for the infiltration of trade unions, Irish language and cultural organisations, and even religious bodies of all persuasions.

University students are to be "indoctrinated".

Most cynical of all, I understand, is the approach to religion in the plan. Sectarianism is to be encouraged with the aim of promoting religious strife and civil disorder.

U.S. House of Representatives, *Hearings before the Subcommittee on Europe of the Committee of Foreign Affairs*, 92nd Congress, 2d sess., Feb. 28 and 29 and Mar. 1, 1972, pp. 242-43.

3.
Nationalist Views

Originally, one of the strengths of the Civil Rights Association was its freedom from the taint of treason. It did not try to end partition, it was simply working to help Catholics gain their rights as British citizens. Perhaps the movement's best-known leader was Bernadette Devlin, who in 1968 was a student at Queen's University, Belfast. Soon after her election in April 1969 (at age twenty-one) to the British Parliament, the civil rights movement lost ground to more violent groups. The most important of these was the Irish Republican Army.

The IRA may be traced back to the Fenians, who were founded in the United States after the Civil War. After the partition of Ireland, the IRA fought against the treaty, and in the late 1930s and early 1940s launched a bombing campaign against England. Twenty years later it started a guerrilla campaign in the rural areas of Northern Ireland, which again failed. The IRA kept trying to unite Ireland partly because it was a romantic movement trying to fulfill an age-old dream. Dominic Behan's haunting song "The Patriot Game" tells of the romance of the IRA, with its memories of atrocities both by the British and by the government of the South.

By the late 1960s, if the romance remained the weapons had at least gone, the IRA having sold them to the Free Welsh Army, a comic opera bunch notable only for blowing themselves up with their own bombs. As the interview with Cathal Goulding shows, the "Official" IRA had become a Marxist organization, more interested in propaganda than in Thompson submachine guns.

Thus, when in late 1968 and early 1969 the civil rights

96

movement provoked a Protestant backlash that threatened a pogrom, many Catholics felt unprotected. "IRA = I ran away" was scrawled on a Belfast wall. In August 1969 Catholics welcomed the British army because they felt it would protect them from Protestant vigilantes. But soon, feeling they must look after themselves, they formed the "Provisional" branch of the IRA, which became involved in an urban guerrilla war against the army and police. So effective did their campaign become that in August 1971 the Government of Northern Ireland invoked the 1922 Special Powers Act, introducing internment of suspected terrorists without trial.

Internment had been very effective in defeating the IRA's rural campaign of the early 1960s, but in 1971 it was a complete political failure. New, more violent leaders replaced those who had been locked up. Police and army methods of interrogating suspects — which, on the basis of considerable evidence, including a British government report, can only be described as torture — inflamed Catholic sentiment. Songs like "The Men behind the Wire" expressed such anger, which was also vented in a campaign of escalating violence. In the two years before internment, 66 people died violently in Northern Ireland, compared to 610 in the following seventeen months.

PLAYBOY INTERVIEW WITH BERNADETTE DEVLIN (SEPTEMBER 1972)*

PLAYBOY: What was it like growing up as a Catholic in Protestant Northern Ireland?

DEVLIN: Well, it was an education in more ways than one. I was born in Cookstown, in County Tyrone, a small farming community that's sort of a microcosm of Ulster. It was originally a plantation, settled by the Scots Presbyterians the British imported in the 17th Century to take over the land from us restless

---

*Excerpts from the *Playboy* interview with Bernadette Devlin. Originally appeared in *Playboy* magazine; copyright © 1972 by *Playboy*.

natives. To this day, the town is divided almost evenly between the descendants of the original Protestant settlers and the Catholics they subjugated; both groups are still segregated in the geographical areas of the town where their ancestors lived 300 years ago. And attitudes haven't changed much, either; the Protestants still have a sense of settler superiority and expect the Catholics to stay in their place and not get uppity, pretty much the way your own American colonists once viewed the Indians, or the way many white Southerners still feel about blacks. And, like the Indians and the blacks, we were poor, virtually disenfranchised and very angry. We still are. . . .

PLAYBOY: As a professional believer in self-determination for all peoples, don't you grant the Northern Protestants the right to remain with Britain, if that's the desire of the majority?

DEVLIN: The partition of Ireland was no more acceptable to far-seeing Irishmen than the secession of your own Southern states was to Abraham Lincoln. If you'd taken a plebiscite within the Confederacy in 1861, you would have found that a majority of Southerners preferred to split off from the United States. Lincoln put the good of the entire country ahead of regional sectarianism, and this led to your Civil War.

PLAYBOY: What happened to Catholics in the North after partition?

DEVLIN: The new Unionist regime made a deliberate decision to drive out as many Roman Catholics as possible in order to increase their numerical majority, which was roughly two to one. Some Catholics packed and headed south. But the overwhelming majority refused to leave. Threats, economic reprisals, violence — all were used against them. Protestant employers fired Catholic employees; those who kept their jobs were harassed by vigilante goon squads. For the military arm of this violence, Stormont, Northern Ireland's Parliament, formed the Royal Ulster Constabulary and the B Specials, whose members were recruited from the most fanatic cadres of the Orange Order. The B Specials carried on the tradition of the Black and Tans, executing Nationalist leaders, burning down Catholic homes — often with the occupants inside — and indiscriminately terrorizing the countryside.

PLAYBOY: Had Catholics no protection under the Law?

DEVLIN: No. It was a legally sanctioned reign of terror. In 1922, Stormont passed the Special Powers Act, which gave the authorities power to arrest people without a warrant on suspicion "of acting or of having acted or of being about to act" in a manner prejudicial to the state — and to hold them for indefinite periods without charge or trial. Under the act, the police had the right to search persons and premises without a judicial warrant, to close roads or bridges, to declare curfews, to prohibit meetings, to arrest any individual who "by word of mouth" spreads false reports or makes false statements, to suppress the circulation of any newspaper, film or gramophone record and to arrest and hold — without trial, habeas corpus or the right to consult a lawyer — anyone doing anything calculated to be "prejudicial to the preservation of the peace or maintenance of order" in Northern Ireland. The act explicitly authorized punishment by flogging for a host of lesser offenses. One of its most relevant provisions is the clause denying an inquest to any prisoner who died while in custody; this was most useful to the B Specials, since they fatally tortured so many of their prisoners.

The Special Powers Act is still in force in Northern Ireland, and during the present troubles, over 1000 people have been interned without trial under its provisions. It's a kind of Magna Charta for tyrants. There isn't a law like it on the books anywhere else in western Europe; even fascist dictatorships like those in Spain and Portugal haven't dared outrage world opinion by passing such unabashedly repressive legislation. When South Africa was debating security measures a few years ago, the South African minister of the interior told Parliament that he would exchange his whole battery of repressive legislation for just one clause of the Special Powers Act. That's the type of law and order we've been living under in the North for 50 years.

PLAYBOY: Most observers will grant that Northern Ireland was set up as a vehicle for Protestant supremacy; but in recent years, the more enlightened Ulster political leaders have recognized the necessity of full Catholic participation in the life of the state. Doesn't violent Catholic resistance, in which you've participated, actually retard progress?

DEVLIN: What you don't seem to understand is that things began to change only *after* we started our resistance, a resistance that began peacefully and grew violent only in the face of persistent Unionist violence against *us*. Until 1968, when we started actively opposing the system, not one iota of reform had been initiated by Stormont. We faced institutionalized discrimination in every area of our life: To be born Catholic was to be born a second-class citizen. Take employment: In Northern Ireland, the unemployment rate is 8 percent of the adult male population, but the overwhelming majority of those without jobs has always been Catholic. In Derry, the figure rises to between 12 and 15 percent; in other Catholic areas, it soars as high as 45 percent.

Practically all the major industry in Northern Ireland is Protestant-controlled and has traditionally followed discriminatory hiring practices. Belfast's biggest single employer, the Harland-Wolff shipyards, has 10,000 workers; 400 of them are Catholics. The situation is just as bad in public employment, which provides a wide range of jobs; most of these positions are filled by local councils; and since Unionist gerrymandering ensures that these are preponderantly Protestant, they tend to award all the good jobs to fellow Protestants. . . .

PLAYBOY: How did the civil rights movement get its start?

DEVLIN: It was formed in 1967 by a group of middle-class Roman Catholics who had been influenced by the progress of the black civil rights movement in your own country. They called the new organization the Northern Ireland Civil Rights Association. At first it restricted itself to investigating individual complaints of public discrimination; but after a year it broadened its program and asked for six reforms. These were simple: one man, one vote; an end to gerrymandering; anti-discrimination legislation; impartial allocation of public housing; repeal of the Special Powers Act; and disbanding of the B Specials. These were eminently reasonable and moderate demands, but their implementation would have had a revolutionary effect on the Northern Irish social structure. It was a revolution that Stormont and the 9 percent of the Protestants who owned 92 percent of the land in Ulster were determined to resist.

PLAYBOY: What was the attitude of the authorities?

DEVLIN: A sort of restrained hostility. Our prime minister at the time was Captain Terence O'Neill, a wealthy Protestant landlord who fancied himself something of a public-relations expert. He was trying to clean up the sectarian image of Ulster without correcting any of its specific injustices. This put him in something of the position of Adolf Hitler commemorating Brotherhood Week, but it fooled a lot of well-meaning people. The civil rights movement caught O'Neill by surprise, and he and his cronies made a crucial mistake: Instead of adopting a tolerant line and throwing out a few sops that might have co-opted the middle-class element, they treated the whole movement as some kind of sinister conspiracy between Dublin and the I.R.A. During the first march, the police behaved properly enough, although they blockaded us from the Protestant part of town; but six weeks later, on October 5, 1968, when the next march was held in Derry, they brutally suppressed it.

PLAYBOY: What happened?

DEVLIN: The same thing that happened during your Chicago Democratic Convention that year: The police went mad. You must understand that Derry has always been the powder keg of Northern Ireland. The city has a tremendous emotional appeal to Protestants. In 1689, it held out against a Catholic siege for 105 days, buying the Protestants time for the eventual victory at the Battle of the Boyne. As a result, Derry became the visible symbol of Protestant courage. But Derry also has a large Catholic majority and some of the worst housing conditions, political repression and unemployment in the country.

I'll never forget the atmosphere in Derry that day. The very air seemed to crackle with emotional electricity. We all had a tremendous feeling of being *alive,* of finally taking a stand for something important, and to hell with the consequences. But we could see right away that the attitude of the Royal Ulster Constabulary was very different from what it had been on the earlier march. We had only moved a few hundred yards before the police came toward us. When we tried to regroup down the side streets, they encircled us. There were hundreds of them, and with no act of physical or verbal violence on our part, they came charging in, swinging their truncheons right and left, kicking and punching everyone in their way. People panicked and started to run, but there was no place to go. I panicked, too. I stood there like a statue, watching people being clubbed all around me. The thing I remember most clearly to this very day is the expression on the faces of the police — their tight thick smiles, their eager eyes. They were *enjoying* it. It was as if they had waited 50 years for this.

PLAYBOY: What was the public reaction to this brutality?

DEVLIN: I think the impact on public opinion was something like what happened after Dr. King's people were beaten up by Bull Connor's policemen on that bridge in Alabama. Suddenly, fair-minded people everywhere could see us being treated like animals. In the aftermath of the violence, I was so furious I could have gone into a police barracks with a machine gun and slaughtered everyone there. But in retrospect, I realize the police had actually done us a great favor. They dramatized our plight to the world. The civil rights movement had started out as a small middle-class pressure group, but it took only one day of police violence to transform it into a mass movement. . . .

PLAYBOY: Your critics have claimed that by refusing to give O'Neill a chance to implement his reforms, your members were responsible for the subsequent violence.

DEVLIN: That's nonsense. First of all, O'Neill's so-called reforms never had a chance to begin with, because they touched only the surface of the sickness in Northern Ireland. O'Neill was like a doctor prescribing aspirin for terminal cancer. And the violence you speak of was all directed *at* us. We were harassed all along the route by roving bands of Paisleyites, and about seven miles outside Derry, we were ambushed by a large crowd of heavily armed Unionists. The police, who were allegedly protecting us, just stood back and let them wade into us, throwing bottles and stones and swinging clubs and crowbars. We were trapped on a field between the river and the Burntollet Bridge. Many marchers were mercilessly beaten and thrown into the water. I saw young girls being hurled off the bridge by Paisleyites, whose accomplices would wait below and beat them with nail-studded clubs when they tried to swim to the bank.

I recognized the futility of running and stood still. One Paisleyite swung a huge plank at me, and I still remember it coming toward my eyes, with two big nails sticking out. I threw my hands across my face and the nails drove into the backs of my hands. Luckily, my reflexes were quick; otherwise, I would have been blinded. Then the man slammed me across the knees and I fell to the ground. Four or five of his mates gathered around me, trying to kick my face in. I curled into a ball, covering my head with my arms, while their boots slammed into me. Finally, they trotted off after a new victim. I lay there a minute or two, then raised my head and looked around. The field was a shambles, with the battered bodies of marchers strewn on the ground like driftwood. It was a miracle nobody died at the Burntollet ambush, but 87 people were admitted to hospitals, many of them seriously injured.

The ambush taught us all we needed to know about the "reformist" government of Terence O'Neill. . . .

PLAYBOY: A period of relative calm had followed the arrival of British troops in 1969. What caused the subsequent escalation of hostilities?

DEVLIN: The British army itself. It's true that when the troops first arrived, many Catholics welcomed their presence and considered them protectors from the police and the armed Orange mob. And I'm sure the average British soldier was a decent enough young fellow, just trying to do his job. When the troops came in, both Stormont and London were treading very carefully. As an emotionally charged concession, Wilson even disarmed and eventually disbanded the B Specials. But slowly and surely, pressure increased in the Catholic ghettos. In June 1970, Wilson was replaced as British prime minister by the Conservative Edward Heath. Whereas Wilson wanted to seduce the Catholics into co-operation, Heath preferred to rape them. Instructions were issued to commanders in the North to take a hard line toward the Catholics.

The turning point was a series of arms searches in the Catholic area of Belfast. A minor incident between soldiers and a few taunting children erupted into a major riot. The military command promptly slapped a curfew on the area and ordered a house-to-house search for concealed weapons. The curfew affected over 15,000 Catholics, and more than 3000 homes were searched. While people choked and wept from the huge amounts of CS gas poured into the area, the troops kicked in doors and smashed and looted many of the houses they searched, roughing up anyone who protested. Residents poured into the streets to demonstrate against this behavior and the troops opened fire: Three Catholics were shot dead and another was crushed to death under an armored car. After that, Catholics understandably began viewing the army as a hostile occupying force. All the good will built up over the past months rapidly disintegrated. . . .

PLAYBOY: What happened on Bloody Sunday?

DEVLIN: Sometimes it's hard to believe it really *did* happen. There were over 20,000 people at Derry that day. The government had declared our gathering illegal, but we were going ahead in defiance of the ban. Twenty or 30 young men were the only ones to make any trouble; they taunted the army and threw some rocks. But that's standard behavior these days and there was no other violence from the crowd; no guns, no petrol bombs, nothing.

Then, without warning, British paratroops charged out and began firing wildly at the crowd — spraying bullets everywhere. They kept on firing for the next 20 minutes. The scene became a nightmare. . . .

As I walked through the streets, I found I knew many of the dead. One young girl had seen soldiers jump out of their armored cars to fire indiscriminately into the crowd. A 17-year-old boy next to her was shot in the stomach; he died with his head in her lap. She went into shock, but a man named Barney McGuigan led her away to safety. As the firing kept on, the two of them heard somebody nearby screaming: "I don't want to die. I don't want to die." McGuigan told the girl he'd have to find that man and help him. She urged him not to, but he said, "No, I must help. Don't worry, I'll wave a white handkerchief. The soldiers wouldn't shoot at a white handkerchief." He walked slowly out to the dying man, waving his handkerchief. As he reached his side, they shot him through the head. All the survivors have stories like that to tell.

When the list was complete, 13 men, half of them in their teens, were dead and another 27 wounded, men and women alike. We just sat there through the night, calling relatives in other parts of the country and saying, "I'm sorry, there's no other way to say this, but your son has just been shot by the British army." When it was all over, we just sat in the corner and cried, and then got drunk. The British army must be very proud of its work that day.

PLAYBOY: Can you see no grounds for reconciliation with England? Or will your bitterness, violence and misery be handed down to the next generation?

DEVLIN: There's a solution to any human problem. In this case, I can actually see two solutions, short term and long term. For the short term, hostilities could cease tomorrow if the British would unconditionally release all internees and other political prisoners, declare an amnesty for all those currently charged with crimes against the state and withdraw all troops to their barracks with a specified date for total withdrawal from Northern Ireland.

Stormont and the whole Unionist state apparatus would have to be permanently dismantled, not just temporarily suspended as it is now, under Westminster's direct rule. All parties in Ireland, Protestant and Catholic, conservative and revolutionary, could then get together to determine conditions for the peaceful reunification of their country and the protection of minority rights. That would be a short-term solution for the immediate suffering and bloodshed. It's far from perfect and it might not work at all, given our hardened sectarian attitudes.

PLAYBOY: If the British were to move out tomorrow, what would be the danger of a Protestant backlash?

DEVLIN: It's highly probable. I believe in times of crisis there are two ways to go — left and right — and the Protestants would probably go right. If they fight, we'll have to defend ourselves. But I don't believe that violence from any quarter is going to radicalize the Protestants; they've got to be radicalized on the class issues. So, for that matter, have the Catholics.

PLAYBOY: But would an independent Ireland be economically viable?

DEVLIN: Yes, but only on socialist lines. For example, if we nationalized the mines, we would release £80,000,000 in the next seven years. The British say we can't live without their money. The British taxpayers pour approximately £150,000,000 into Northern Ireland every year. But we export £700,000,000 of profit from Northern Ireland to Britain in the same period.

PLAYBOY: Wouldn't you lose those export markets if the relationship with England were severed?

DEVLIN: Why would we? We make the produce and sell it; we could sell it anywhere. We've got stuff that can be eaten, can be worn, can be bought. It's a great myth that without capitalism nothing can be bought or sold. Henry Ford personally doesn't have a clue how to build motorcars, how to sell them, how to repair them. But he's got all the money because his grandfather invented the motorcar. By accident of birth, Henry Ford continues to live on the work of other people. Everything England made and every penny she has taken out of this country, she made out of us. She stole the wealth beneath the ground, she stole the wealth above it, she stole the wealth of our labor. And she came here to do just that. If we keep all we have, we'll survive. There's no doubt about that.

So you see, the ultimate long-range solution for Ireland, which I realize won't come about overnight, is independent socialism. Until we have a society in which we solve our own economic and social problems and control our own destiny, the present problems of exploitation and injustice will remain. That's why I'm a committed socialist and why more and more of our people are turning toward socialism as the only viable alternative. We can't have true freedom without social justice; and in Ireland, we can't have either without socialism. It won't come today, tomorrow or the day after. But it will come. It *has* to come.

PLAYBOY: In the light of all this hatred and bloodshed, are you really optimistic about the future of Ireland?

DEVLIN: Yes, I am. We've been fighting 800 years to bring a just system to this country, and for 800 years they've jailed us. Today our spirit is stronger than ever. I'm still here, and thousands of kids are growing up just like me. I've brought a child of my own into this world, and I'm convinced she'll live to see the society we're trying to build. If not, her children will. If you dream a dream long enough, it becomes reality. Our dream is coming. Nothing can stop it.

Playboy, XIX (September 1972), pp. 67ff.

IRA SONG: "THE PATRIOT GAME" (1957)

Come all you young rebels and list while I sing,
For love of one's land is a terrible thing.
It banishes fear with the speed of a flame
And makes us all part of the patriot game.

My name is O'Hanlon, I'm just gone sixteen,
My home is in Monaghan, there I was weaned.
I was taught all my life cruel England to blame
And so I'm a part of the patriot game.

'Tis barely two years since I wandered away
With the local battalion of the bold IRA.
I read of our heroes and wanted the same
To play up my part in the patriot game.

They told me how Connolly was shot in a chair,
His wounds from the battle all bleeding and bare,
His fine body twisted, all battered and lame;
They soon made him part of the patriot game.

I joined a battalion from dear Bally Bay
And gave up my boyhood so happy and gay
For now as a soldier I'd drill and I'd train
To play my full part in the patriot game.

This Ireland of mine has for long been half free,
Six counties are under John Bull's tyranny.
And still De Valera is greatly to blame
For shirking his part in the patriot game.

I don't mind a bit if I shoot down police;
They're lackeys for war, never guardians of peace;
But yet as deserters I'm never let aim
Those rebels who sold out the patriot game.

And now as I lie with my body all holes
I think of those traitors who bargained and sold;
I'm sorry my rifle has not done the same
For the quisling who sold out the patriot game.

Sing Out, X, (Summer 1960), p. 12.

INTERVIEW WITH CATHAL GOULDING CHIEF OF STAFF, "OFFICIAL" IRA (19 AUGUST 1970)

QUESTION: Do you see any similarity between the struggle of the Vietnamese people to win control of their own country and the present fight of the Irish people to expel foreign occupiers and defeat or win over their native allies?

ANSWER: I certainly do. The first similarity is that when the French empire was weakening and the French were being forced out of Vietnam, the American imperialists came in to replace them.

That is, imperialism is international. International financiers and international speculators have developed interests in all the colonies, whether British, French, or any other. The same thing has happened in Ireland.

The same thing might happen to us here in Ireland as happened in Vietnam. The British empire is disintegrating and it is not so fantastic to imagine that if the British were driven out that the Americans might move in to replace them.

The Americans already have bases in Derry and other places in the Six Counties and I believe that they would support imperialist rule here if we were strong enough to beat the British.

QUESTION: Will there be any separation in time between the national and social revolutions?

ANSWER: I think that in the future the revolution, or the fight to establish national independence, must develop toward a fight to establish the ordinary people in the ownership of Ireland.

If we don't have a programme and a policy to bring about such a development, we are only wasting our time. We don't intend to exchange foreign capitalist exploitation for native *gombeen* [money lender] capitalist exploitation. Therefore, at some stage the struggle for national liberation must develop toward the establishment of the people in the ownership of Ireland, that is, toward a struggle to establish a socialist republic.

QUESTION: Which social class do you think will play the leading role in liberating the country from British imperialism?

ANSWER: The class that always plays the leading role in any national liberation struggle is the working class, the people of no property, the landless people, the industrial workers in the city, and the very small peasant farmer.

These are the people who have traditionally supported the national liberation movements in Ireland all through the centuries.

Rich people were never interested in national liberation. They are already liberated. They have theirs. Only the ordinary people, the people of no property, are incorruptible. They have nothing to lose.

QUESTION: Do you see any similarities between the struggle of the nationalist population in Northern Ireland and that of the American black people?

ANSWER: The fight of the nationalist people in the Six Counties is very much like that of the American Negroes. For instance, the Negro is a second-class citizen in the United States; so also is the nationalist in the Six Counties. If a Nationalist and a Unionist go forward for a job, no matter what qualifications the Nationalist has, the Unionist will get the job.

The same sort of thing happens in the United States. Segregated schools are second-class schools. The best teachers go to the best schools and the best schools are given to whites. The same sort of thing is happening in the Six Counties.

QUESTION: What lessons do you think that nationalists of Northern Ireland can draw from the struggle of the American black people?

ANSWER: The first lesson that the people of the Six Counties learned from the American Negro was that they could not get anything unless they organized and demonstrated to demand their rights. When we helped to initiate the civil-rights movement in Northern Ireland we copied to a great extent the approach and activities of the Negro people in America.

On the other hand, I think the Negro people in America, those militant groups which have now moved beyond civil rights, could have learned something from us. We always had a military organization, a movement that could use physical force against the establishment.

QUESTION: How do you propose to approach the problem of the military occupation of Northern Ireland, within the context of Ireland as a whole, and internationally? Do you favor a worldwide campaign for the withdrawal of British troops from Northern Ireland?

ANSWER: We do favor such a campaign and we are trying to develop one particularly through our allies in America, the people who are organizing the different Irish emigrant groups in America. We are trying to get these people to do as much work as possible to publicize why the British troops are in Ireland, what they are doing and what they are protecting. We have Irish organizations in Australia, New Zealand, America, and England. We have also established contact with other countries where there are socialist groups and we are trying to work with these people to arouse worldwide feeling against the occupation of Ireland by England.

But I believe the job of pushing the British troops out of Ireland will eventually have to be done by ourselves.

QUESTION: Do you think that the military organization of your movement is compatible with full internal democracy, democratic discussion of policy?

ANSWER: Yes. Our movement is basically a revolutionary movement. We are not organized like, say, the American army or the British army. Our military organization has annual conferences which set the basic policy. Resolutions come from units all over the country and from ordinary members. The officers appointed to run the headquarters staff of the Irish Republican Army are elected by the members. So our military organization is basically a workers' army.

It is an army in which the working class and the small farmers have a say in the policy. They have a say in what our tactic or strategy is going to be for each year, and they also have a say in who should lead the army. The man who may be chief of staff one year could be an ordinary soldier the next.

In Gerry Foley, *Ireland in Rebellion* (New York: Pathfinder Press, 1971), pp. 20–25.

"THE MEN BEHIND THE WIRE," A PROTEST SONG AGAINST INTERNMENT (1972)

Through the little streets of Belfast
In the dark of early morn'
British soldiers came marauding
Wrecking little homes with scorn
Heedless of the crying children
Dragging fathers from their beds
Beating sons while helpless mothers
Watch the blood flow from their heads.

Armoured cars, and tanks and guns
Came to take away our sons
But every man will stand behind
The men behind the wire.

Not for them a judge or jury
Or indeed a crime at all
Being Irish means they're guilty
So we're guilty one and all
Round the world the truth will echo
Cromwell's men are here again
England's name again is sullied
In the eyes of honest men.

Armoured cars, and tanks and guns
Came to take away our sons
But every man will stand behind
The men behind the wire.

Proudly march behind our banners
Firmly stand behind our men
We will have them free to help us
Build a nation once again
On the people, stand together
Proudly, firmly on your way
Never fear and never falter
Till the boys are home to stay.

Armoured cars, and tanks and guns
Came to take away our sons
But every man will stand behind
The men behind the wire.

Written by Pat McGuigan while he was interned in Long
Kesh (Glenside Music Publishing Co.: Dublin, 1972).

4.
An American View

Ever since the famine of the 1840s forced nearly a million Irish to flee to the United States the Irish problem has bedeviled Anglo-American relations; and Irish Americans have supported nationalist movements in the Old Country. Memories of the famine, of horrendous voyages across the Atlantic, and of their ancestors' fight to "make it" in the New World still prompt many otherwise conservative — even anti-Communist — Irish Americans to contribute money and occasionally arms to the IRA, whose "official" wing is openly Marxist. Of course, Senator Kennedy is neither an extremist nor a gunrunner, but — as with many of his fellow Irish Americans — the experiences of the past and of his family have influenced his views on Northern Ireland.

SENATE SPEECH OF SENATOR EDWARD KENNEDY (20 OCTOBER 1971)

Mr. President, I am pleased to join with Senator Abraham Ribicoff in introducing a Senate resolution calling for the immediate withdrawal of British troops from Northern Ireland and the establishment of a united Ireland.

We believe that the resolution states the only realistic means to end the killing in Northern Ireland, and to bring peace to a land that has given so much to America, a land that has done so much to enrich the history of our own Nation, a land that is suffering so deeply today.

The conscience of America cannot keep silent when men and women of Ireland are dying. Britain has lost its way, and the innocent people of Northern Ireland are the ones who now must suffer. The time has come for Americans of every faith and political persuasion to speak out. We owe ourselves and our sacred heritage no less.

Down through the centuries, the people of Ireland have been forced to wage a continuing and arduous struggle for freedom and equality. For generations, division and despair have scarred the countryside. The ancient right of self-determination has been denied. Often alone, often without notice from others throughout the world, brave men and women of Ireland have given their lives for the principles they hold dear. Millions have been driven from their homes, forced to leave the land they love, obliged to seek a new life in nations where the yoke of repression could not reach.

As President Kennedy liked to say, America is a nation of immigrants. The Irish yield to none in their contributions to the people and culture of America. The waves of Irish immigrants who sought our shores in the 19th century launched a movement that spanned our continent and changed the course of American history. They say today that Irish blood flows in the veins of one out of every seven Americans. There are more Irishmen in America now than in the Ireland they left behind.

The Irish have had a monumental impact on the America we know today. Wherever we look — in business and the labor movement, in literature and music, in science and religion — and above all in public services at every level of government, we find citizens of Irish descent who helped to make our Nation great.

They built our railroads, dug our coal, erected our buildings and our churches. They organized our unions and our businesses. They fought in all our wars.

The heart of the solution we offer today is the call for immediate withdrawal of British troops from Ulster and the establishment of a united Ireland. Without a firm commitment to troop withdrawal and unification, there can be no peace in Northern Ireland. The killing will go on, and the intolerable mounting violence will continue.

To those who say that the inevitable result of a troop withdrawal will be a blood bath in Northern Ireland, I reply that the blood is upon us now, and the bath is growing more bloody every week. As the resolution states, the only hope for peace is the prompt return of law enforcement to local civilian control in Ulster, in accord with procedures acceptable to all the parties.

It is equally clear that the true answer to these other issues is the unification of Ireland, the overall goal we seek in our Senate resolution. America learned a century ago that our Nation, divided against itself, could not stand. The question now for Ireland is whether the people there will accept that lesson without enduring a civil war like our own. I believe deeply that they will. In 1918, the people of Ireland voted 81 percent in favor of an independent Republic. If only the cruel and constant irritation of the British military presence is withdrawn, Ireland can be whole again.

Some have urged that the only route for Britain out of Ulster is the solution used by President De Gaulle to end the Algerian war. Just as De Gaulle opened the arms of France to welcome home those Frenchmen who felt they could not live in a free Algeria, so, it is urged, Britain could open its arms to any Protestants in Ulster who feel they could not live in a united Ireland.

But I do not believe that such a solution will be necessary, at least on any wholesale scale for the Protestants who live in Ulster now. It is far more likely that, once the commitment to unification is made, the 500,000 Catholics and 1 million Protestants of Ulster will work together in a new Ireland, to create the sort of political and social arrangements under which both can live and work in peace together, with full and mutual respect for the rights of all. Anyone who doubted that truth need only examine the extraordinary record of equality, tolerance, and religious freedom compiled by the overwhelming 2.7 million Catholic majority in the Republic of Ireland toward the 300,000 Protestant minority there.

In addition to the calls for the withdrawal of British troops and the establishment of a united Ireland, there are four other major actions that our Senate resolution proposes:

First, there must be an end to the current internment policy and the simultaneous release of all the prisoners who have been arrested and imprisoned under that brutal and arbitrary policy.

Second, the resolution calls for full respect for the civil rights of all the people of Northern Ireland, and the end of all political, social, economic, and religious discrimination that now exists in Ulster.

Third, the resolution calls for implementation of the many basic reforms promised by the Government of Great Britain and Northern Ireland since 1968, including the reforms specifically promised in the area of law enforcement, housing, employment, and voting rights.

Fourth, and finally, the resolution calls for the dissolution of the Parliament of Northern Ireland. Today, the Parliament of Northern Ireland has become one of the overriding symbols of oppression of the Ulster minority. For generations, the Parliament at Stormont has been the tool of Protestant domination in Ulster, and I can find no justification for its continuance. Instead, pending the overall settlement of the Ulster issue, the people of Northern Ireland should be governed directly from Westminster — the British Parliament in London — just like every other British subject.

We believe that the sum of these proposals offers the only real hope for the freedom of the people of Northern Ireland and an end to the reign of violence and terror that threatens to consume that land. No one doubts that Ireland stands today on the brink of a massive civil war. The specter we face is nothing less than the senseless destruction of Ireland herself. No American who loves Ireland or who remembers her proud and noble history can stand silent in the face of the tragedy and horror now unfolding in Ulster.

Ireland has given much to America, and we owe her much in return.

Congressional Record, CXVII, part 28, 3672-73.

5.
A Southern View

When in March 1972 an American journalist asked Prime Minister Lynch of the Irish Republic to comment on Senator Kennedy's call for the withdrawal of British troops from Northern Ireland, he replied: "I don't think he understands the situation as fully as we do." Prime Minister Lynch's response was significant because it represented a major shift in the stance of the Irish Republic. In the past, whenever the IRA was weak, and reunification remote, Irish politicians could always win votes by attacking partition. Yet whenever the IRA became effective in the North it also became a threat to the government of the South, which moved against it, interning its leaders and cutting off its bases on the Southern side of the border. Moreover, during the last decade relations between Ireland and Britain have improved. Both find the religious hatreds of the past increasingly archaic and, after both joined the European Common Market in 1973, international frontiers even more irrelevant.

This does not mean that the South has given up its dream of a united Ireland. Rather, it has kept that goal but jettisoned the bombastic rhetoric of the past, realizing, as Prime Minister Lynch's speech suggests, that before reunification can be achieved the South must make compromises and change the direction of much of its history since partition.

SPEECH OF JACK LYNCH, PRIME MINISTER OF THE REPUBLIC OF IRELAND (1969)

I would like in clear and simple terms to set out the basis of our thinking and policy. I hope that this will help to reduce those tensions in the North which arise from misunderstandings or apprehensions about our attitude or intentions.

The historical and natural unity of Ireland was also a political unity until this was artificially sundered by the Government of Ireland Act passed by the British Government in 1920. The Act, in effect, provided for the partitioning of Ireland and the creation of a Government of Northern Ireland subordinate to Westminster. Partition was not expected to be permanent even by the authors of this statute — the ultimate aim of "one Parliament and one Government for the whole of Ireland" appeared in the official summary of the Bill preceding this legislation and provision was made for a Council of Ireland which, according as powers were transferred to it by the two parts of Ireland, might develop into an All-Ireland Parliament.

Mr. Asquith, former British Prime Minister, said:

"Ireland is a nation; not two nations, but one nation. There are few cases in history, and as a student of history in a humble way, I myself know none, of a nationality at once so distinct, so persistent, and so assimilative as the Irish."

Mr. Winston Churchill once said:

> Whatever Ulster's right may be, she cannot stand in the way of the whole of the rest of Ireland. Half a province cannot impose a permanent veto on the nation. Half a province cannot obstruct forever the reconciliation between the British and the Irish democracies and deny all satisfaction to the united wishes of the British Empire.

King George V, speaking in Belfast at the opening of the Northern Ireland Parliament in June, 1921, hoped that the opening would be:

the prelude of the day in which the Irish people, North and South, under one Parliament or two, as those Parliaments may themselves decide, shall work together in common love for Ireland upon the sure foundation of mutual justice and respect.

I need not explain or justify the fundamental desire of the overwhelming majority of the people of this island for the restoration in some form of its national unity. This desire is not confined to Irishmen of any particular creed or ancestry. I want to make it clear, however, once more, that we have no intention of using force to realise this desire. I said as recently as 28th August that it was and has been the Government's policy to seek the re-unification of the country by peaceful means.

The unity we seek is not something forced but a free and genuine union of those living in Ireland based on mutual respect and tolerance and guaranteed by a form or forms of government authority in Ireland providing for progressive improvement of social, economic and cultural life in a just and peaceful environment.

Of its nature this policy — of seeking unity through agreement in Ireland between Irishmen — is a long-term one. It is no less, indeed it is even more, patriotic for that. Perseverance in winning the respect and confidence of those now opposed to unity must be sustained by goodwill, patience, understanding and, at times, forbearance.

The terrible events of the past few months have made it evident to all that, apart from disrupting the unity of Ireland, the 1920 devolution of powers has not provided a system of government, acceptable as fair and just, to many of the people in Northern Ireland. I need not detail these events nor refer to recent objective appraisals of that system of government. But change there obviously must be. We are concerned that the grievances of so many of our fellow Irishmen and women be quickly remedied and their fears set at rest. We also have a legitimate concern regarding the disposition to be made by the British Government in relation to the future administration of Northern Ireland. Our views on how peace and justice can be assured in this small island are relevant and entitled to be heard.

Let me make it clear, too, that in seeking re-unification, our aim is not to extend the domination of Dublin. We have many times down the years expressed our willingness to seek a solution on federal lines and in my most recent statement I envisaged the possibility of intermediate stages in an approach to the final agreed solution.

Whatever the constitutional setting might be — and we are prepared to explore all the possibilities in constructive discussion — the united Ireland we desire is one in which there would be a scrupulously fair deal for all. The Protestants of the North need have no fear of any interference with their religious freedom or civil liberties and rights.

Differences in political outlook or religious belief need not set people apart. They exist in most countries and are no barrier to effective and constructive co-operation of the various elements in the community in national development. Indeed, diversity of cultural background can exert a stimulating influence. The real barriers are those created by fear, suspicion and intolerance.

Every responsible person must hope that early and adequate reforms will bring peace and security to the people of the North of Ireland so that they may live together in neighbourliness without fear, sharing fairly in improving social and economic conditions, and with fading memories of past dissensions.

It will remain our most earnest aim and hope to win the consent of the majority of the people in the Six Counties to means by which North and South can come together in a re-united and sovereign Ireland earning international respect both for the fairness and efficiency with which it is administered and for its contributions to world peace and progress.

Finally, a few words on recognition. It is quite unreasonable for any Unionist to expect my Government, or any future Government, to abandon the belief and hope that Ireland should be re-united. It is unnecessary to repeat that we seek re-unification by peaceful means. We are not seeking to overthrow by violence the Stormont Parliament or Government but rather to win the agreement of a sufficient number of people in the North to an acceptable form of re-unification. In any case the Stormont Government, being the executive instrument of a subordinate parliament, cannot receive formal international recognition.

It is also, for similar reasons, unreasonable and unnecessary to expect those living in the Six Counties who share our desire for unity to renounce their deepest hopes. We and they have accepted as a practical matter the existence of a government in the North of Ireland exercising certain powers devolved on it by the British Parliament. We have had many fruitful contacts with that Government in matters of mutual concern. I hope that this co-operation between North and South will continue.

May I conclude by referring to the words of Lord Craigavon, the first Prime Minister of Northern Ireland, when he said:

> In this island, we cannot live always separated from one another. We are too small to be apart or for the Border to be there for all time.

John Lynch, *Irish Unity, Northern Ireland, Anglo-Irish Relations, August 1969–October 1971* (Dublin: Government Information Bureau, 1971), pp. 9–12.

6.
British Views

The army is the most obvious British influence in Northern Ireland, where roughly 14,000 regular troops are supported by some 5,000 police and by as many members of the Ulster Defense Regiment, a national guard unit. Everywhere one goes in Ulster there are troops. Armored Land Rovers with rifle-carrying soldiers riding shotgun, armored trucks (known as "pigs"), and scout cars are a constant sight in downtown Belfast, where troops search pedestrians who wish to pass through the barricades that protect the shopping areas.

The British army is a small, all-volunteer force. As the following letter from one of its officers suggests, it is a highly professional organization, fully sensitive to the political ramifications of its role. Many would argue that in responding to terrorist attacks the army has acted with restraint. Yet within a few months of its introduction the army was virtually at war with those people whom it had intended to protect. Historically, the army has always been the enemy of the Nationalists. By attacking the army and provoking military reactions, such as arms searches — which the people whose houses were searched felt was done with unnecessary vigor — the IRA was able to restore the traditional enmity.

More important, many Catholics, wanting change, perceived the army, which was striving to maintain law and order, as the guardians of the status quo and thus of the Protestant establishment. The most damaging blow to the army's reputation and its relationship with the Catholic community came in Derry on "Bloody Sunday," 30 January 1972, when without sufficient justification men of the Para-

126

chute Regiment opened fire on a demonstration against internment and killed 13 people.

While this reminds one of the shooting at Kent State University, British military involvement with Ulster has produced nothing like the domestic turmoil that Vietnam engendered in the United States. Not even the IRA's bombing campaign in England has been able to arouse British public opinion from its basic indifference toward the civil war in Northern Ireland. No draftees have been killed there; no reserve units have been mobilized to patrol the streets of Belfast. Ulster's seventeenth-century passions stir few responsive chords in twentieth-century Britain, while in this age of intercontinental nuclear missiles Ireland has lost the strategic importance it once possessed. Because all three major British political parties basically agree on policy toward Northern Ireland, the issue has stimulated little partisan debate. Since the start of the troubles in 1968, British public opinion has been far more concerned with the European Common Market, the power of the trade unions, unemployment, and (above all) inflation.

This does not mean that the British public has no views on Northern Ireland but, rather, that this is a subject to which few of them are deeply and uncompromisingly committed. If asked, most Britons would say the army should get out of Ulster and let the bloody Irish kill each other instead of shooting British soldiers. After all, Ulster would not be the first colony from which the British have scuttled, and no country like Britain, on the verge of bankruptcy, can afford the billion dollars a year that Northern Ireland costs the taxpayer. As the *New Statesman* editorial suggests, many Englishmen are afraid of being dragged into a Vietnam-like morass.

Largely because of this lack of public and partisan debate, the British government's Ulster policy has remained remarkably consistent. Less than a week after it had committed troops, Her Majesty's government spelled out its basic aims in the Downing Street Declaration of 19 August 1969: to protect the civil rights of the Catholic minority while assuring the Protestant majority that they would not be forced to join the South against their will. The means the government has employed to achieve its ends, however, have changed. At first, working through the Stormont, Westminster relied on military tactics, including the blunder of internment, on which the Stormont had insisted — against the advice of the army. In March 1973, realizing that Northern Ireland's government was politically bankrupt, London dissolved Stormont and introduced direct rule. Since then Her Majesty's government has been publishing "white papers," trying to introduce a new form of government into Northern Ireland by a coalition of center parties in which the two faiths would share power.

So far all such attempts have failed because Ulster is too polarized. Any compromise that is acceptable to one side is anathema to the other.

LETTER FROM A BRITISH ARMY OFFICER ON DUTY IN BELFAST (EARLY 1973)

Battalion Operations Room,
Belfast,
3.45 in the morning.

DEAR HARRY:

Frankly I have found this tour in Belfast has gone extremely fast. The role of the Community Relations Officer in this part of Belfast is somewhat thankless, because the success of one's work can only be realised by the amount of communication between the community and the security forces, and, of course, the decreasing number of incidents involving the security forces. Obviously there are many factors involved towards improving relationships, of which the intelligence war takes precedence. We have managed to send 18 men away behind bars out of the 268 we have had in for questioning, and 55 arrested in the last three months. This may not sound much, but it is very difficult to get a prosecution. We have also found 658 lbs. of gelignite and 12 weapons of various calibers.

Since Xmas it has been very quiet in our area with only minor incidents. We consider that the IRA Provos are furiously trying to re-organize without much success. Frankly, our real

worry is the rise of the extreme elements of the Ulster Defense
Association [a Protestant private army], who have been flexing
their muscles in the same way as the IRA in 1969. They have a
peculiar way of showing their loyalty to the crown by parading in
masks carrying truncheons purely to intimidate the moderates
before the publication of the White Paper.

We await the publication of the White Paper with bated
breath. It cannot satisfy everyone, so there is bound to be trouble.
For every week there is a delay in publication, matters grow
worse. There can be no military solution in an urban guerrilla
situation so complex as this. All we can do is create the right
climate for a political one. If there is any time for this solution, I
would say it is now, so if Westminster decides to put back the
White Paper until May or June, then a golden opportunity will
be lost, because Northern Ireland's silly season begins in June/
July with the marches.

with best wishes,

ADRIAN.

Private correspondence in author's possession (names and
places have been altered).

"ULSTER — OUR VIETNAM?" (1971)

Unless the Labour Opposition wakes up and does its duty,
this government will soon turn Ulster into our Vietnam. We shall
be unable to extricate ourselves from an unwinnable civil war
which corrupts our political morals and destroys our army as a
fighting force. The real tragedy of Vietnam was that the Americans did not will it: they slithered into it. Indeed they hardly knew
they were at war until it was too late to withdraw "without
dishonor" and "without breach of faith." Much the same is
happening to us now in Northern Ireland. Already the shooting
of a couple of soldiers a week is no longer rated front-page news:
it has become part of the normal process of "upholding law and

order" in Northern Ireland. Internment without trial, which
shocked us a few weeks ago, is now accepted as part of that same
process. To judge by their previous facility for blind acquies-
cence, the government will soon be defending the methods of our
investigators in the camps as "inevitable in the circumstances."
The most deadly disease of British and American democracy is the
way we acclimatize ourselves to the evils done in out-of-the-way
places on our behalf. The British army is now occupying Ulster
and waging the Orangeman's war against the IRA. Like the
Kennedy/Johnson Administration our government has announced that the enemy must first be beaten; when that has been
achieved they will consider a political settlement. But in order to
smash the IRA we should have to cut off the supply of arms. We
do not have the troops to close the border with the Irish Republic
any more than the Americans had to seal off South Vietnam. As
for gunrunning, the first planeload of Communist arms was
discovered in Amsterdam this week. But before we succumb to an
orgy of self-congratulation we should remember that, both in
Palestine and the Canal Zone where the Czechs supplied the arms
to Jewish and Egyptian terrorists, our counter-measures failed.
There is no reason to think that they would be more successful in
the northern province of an island which most Irishmen deeply
feel belongs to them.

That is why the government's policy of beating the IRA and
then making a peace settlement is completely impractical. The
very existence of Stormont precludes a discussion of the Irish
problem in anything but Ulster loyalist terms. On that basis,
since the IRA has the active support of the Communist world and
the passive support of the Eire government and people, there is no
reason why the fighting should ever stop.

The Labour Party cannot shrug off its responsibilities by
being marginally more squeamish than the government as each
stage of the crisis develops. Nor is it any use piously asking for
all-Ireland conferences which everyone knows will never be
convened. The situation cries out for an alternative strategy. The
British people want to get out of this mess. There is now no tidy
and painless way backwards, but there is a bold alternative
available if the Labour Party has the courage and sagacity to
proclaim it.

The *New Statesman* has urged before that we should take a firm decision to withdraw the army within a year. Present policies give no hope of a political settlement and a radical change of policy is at least worth a try. Stormont must go to make way for one year of rule from Westminster, whose purpose would be to force the hostile factions into compromise under threat of army withdrawal.

Such a suggestion sounds draconian and immediately it is made hands are thrown up in horror. It is not democratic, it would cause ill-feeling and worst of all it would lead to blood-letting. So say the critics. But what they do not face is the hopelessness of the present situation and the worse horrors soon to come.

As we know from long experience overseas, the British army is not immune to the pressures of a situation that would corrupt, demoralise and brutalise any army in the world. Fighting in Ulster is the usual dirty business — which our troops have grown to detest — when they have to police two hostile communities. On the other occasions they have had hopes of a speedy release from the ordeal. If the army is told that it must garrison Ulster for a prolonged period then it will start to hit back at the terrorists by copying some of their methods. Fighting fire with fire will become the justification for tactics beyond any humane defense. Surely it was the signs that such a thing was beginning to happen and a resolution that it should go no further that brought us out of India and Palestine, Cyprus and Aden.

It is hypocritical to pretend that the army can be left in Ulster without a gradual depletion of its morale and degeneration in its methods. At the very least a change in policy would spare us the shame and grief of Americans as they discover more and more about how the Vietnam war was fought. But a new policy offers more than that. Irishmen would be given a choice. Come what may at the end of one year the British army would withdraw. During that year the Irish could co-operate in establishing a settlement if they chose. They would clearly understand the consequences of not doing so. Failing a settlement, when the army left there would be civil war. It would be a Palestine situation. We believe the great majority do not want that. The Labour Party should advocate a daring course that gives Irishmen, freed from the need to posture, a chance to opt for moderation.

New Statesman, 22 October 1971.

THE DOWNING STREET DECLARATION
(19 August 1969)

1. The United Kingdom Government re-affirm that nothing which has happened in recent weeks in Northern Ireland derogates from the clear pledges made by successive United Kingdom Governments that Northern Ireland should not cease to be a part of the United Kingdom without the consent of the people of Northern Ireland or from the provision in Section 1 of the Ireland Act 1949 that in no event will Northern Ireland or any part thereof cease to be part of the United Kingdom without the consent of the Parliament of Northern Ireland. The Border is not an issue.

2. The United Kingdom Government again affirm that responsibility for affairs in Northern Ireland is entirely a matter of domestic jurisdiction. The United Kingdom Government will take full responsibility for asserting this principle in all international relationships.

3. The United Kingdom Government have ultimate responsibility for the protection of those who live in Northern Ireland when, as in the past week, a breakdown of law and order has occurred. In this spirit, the United Kingdom Government responded to the requests of the Northern Ireland Government for military assistance in Londonderry and Belfast in order to restore law and order. They emphasise again that troops will be withdrawn when law and order has been restored.

4. The Northern Ireland Government have been informed that troops have been provided on a temporary basis in accordance with the United Kingdom's ultimate responsibility. In the context of the commitment of these troops, the Northern Ireland Government have reaffirmed their intention to take into the

fullest account at all times the views of Her Majesty's Government in the United Kingdom, especially in relation to matters affecting the status of citizens of that part of the United Kingdom and their equal rights and protection under the law.

5. The United Kingdom Government have welcomed the decisions of the Northern Ireland Government in relation to Local Government Franchise, the revision of Local Government areas, the allocation of houses, the creation of a Parliamentary Commissioner for Administration in Northern Ireland and machinery to consider citizens' grievances against other public authorities which the Prime Minister reported to the House of Commons at Westminster following his meeting with Northern Ireland Ministers on 21 May as demonstrating the determination of the Northern Ireland Government that there shall be full equality of treatment for all citizens. Both Governments have agreed that it is vital that the momentum of internal reform should be maintained.

6. The two Governments at their meeting at 10 Downing Street today have re-affirmed that in all legislation and executive decisions of Government every citizen of Northern Ireland is entitled to the same equality of treatment and freedom from discrimination as obtains in the rest of the United Kingdom, irrespective of political views or religion. In their future meetings the two Governments will be guided by these mutually accepted principles.

7. Finally, both Governments are determined to take all possible steps to restore normality to the Northern Ireland community so that economic development can proceed at the faster rate which is vital for social stability.

Downing Street Declaration (London: H.M.S.O., 1969), Cmnd. 4154.

7.

Possible Solutions

B efore assessing the feasibility of any solution to the Ulster crisis, we must ask ourselves one question: Does history leave any room for moderation, compromise, or reconciliation, or are the hatreds generated by the past so intense that the only workable solution is one in which the winner takes all?

The latter is implied in two solutions that have been advanced: the IRA's goal of a united socialist Ireland and the Protestant extremists' demands for a return to dominance by the sectarian majority. To a large extent, the likelihood of a winner-take-all solution depends on how past and present hatreds are maintained in the future. The children's songs from Belfast (sung while skipping rope) suggest that historical hatreds may continue for another generation at least.

Other solutions, such as those for a confederate state of all Ireland, wherein the British would guarantee the rights of the Protestant minority, demand concession and compromise. So too does the Sunningdale Agreement, worked out after painstaking negotiations by the British and Irish governments and by Ulster's moderate political parties in December 1973. Yet this agreement, signed just before Christmas, did not survive to Whitsun, because in May 1974 a massive general strike of Protestant workers toppled the new Northern Ireland Executive.

The Sunningdale Agreement, like every other proposal for conciliation, federation, power sharing or compromise, assumed that the vast majority of the people of Northern Ireland are moderates, who are sick of violence and want nothing more than a return to peace. Stop a man in the street, say in Belfast, and he will tell you he wants peace (one would hardly expect — or want — him to say he favors violence). Yet might it not be that most people in Northern Ireland, on both sides, want peace on their own terms of total victory, and that the assumption of a vast majority of moderates is a myth? Certainly it is hard to discern a sizable moderate vote in any of the elections of 1973 or 1974. If this is so, neither a solution imposed internally by Protestant or Catholic extremists, nor based on compromise, would be as satisfactory as one imposed externally by some third power.

Kenneth McCallion argues that the whole Northern Ireland problem be turned over to the United Nations, presumably on the grounds that the British presence is the disruptive element. Left to their own, with a disinterested blue-helmeted umpire ensuring fair play, the Irish will be able to work out their differences among themselves. But R. A. Bruce would not agree. He believes that the two sides will never get along, and only through the drastic means of redrawing the border and forcibly moving people can peace return to Ireland.

Perhaps the last word should go to Dr. Conor Cruise O'Brien, the distinguished Irish historian and politician — not because he provides a solution but because he sketches out the worst and best scenarios for the future. In doing so he suggests how high the stakes are for Ireland in trying to escape the legacy of its past.

BELFAST CHILDREN'S SONGS

If I had a penny,
Do you know what I would do?
I would buy a rope
And hang the Pope,
And let King Billy through.

St. Patrick's Day will be jolly and gay,
And we'll kick all the Protestants out of the way,
If that won't do, we'll cut them in two,
And send them to Hell with their red, white and blue.

Newsweek, 19 April 1971, p. 49.

SUNNINGDALE AGREEMENT
(10 DECEMBER 1973)

1. The conference between the British and Irish Governments and the Parties involved in the Northern Ireland Executive (designate) met at Sunningdale on 6, 7, 8 and 9 December, 1973.

2. During the Conference, each delegation stated their position on the status of Northern Ireland.

3. The Taoiseach [Prime Minister Lynch] said that the basic principle of the conference was that the participants had tried to see what measure of agreement of benefit to all the people concerned could be secured. In doing so, all had reached accommodation with one another on practical arrangements. But none had compromised and none had asked others to compromise in relation to basic aspirations. The people of the Republic, together with a minority in Northern Ireland as represented by the SDLP [Social Democratic Labor Party] delegation, continued to uphold the aspiration towards a united Ireland. The only unity they wanted to see was a unity established by consent.

4. Mr. Brian Faulkner said that delegates from Northern Ireland came to the conference as representatives of apparently incompatible sets of political aspirations who had found it possible to reach agreement to join together in government because each accepted that in doing so they were not sacrificing principles or aspirations. The desire of the majority of the people of Northern Ireland to remain part of the United Kingdom, as represented by the Unionist and Alliance delegations, remained firm.

5. The Irish Government fully accepted and solemnly declared that there could be no change in the status of Northern Ireland until a majority of the people of Northern Ireland desired a change in that status. The British Government solemnly declared that it was, and would remain, their policy to support the wishes of the majority of the people of Northern Ireland. The present status of Northern Ireland is that it is part of the United

Kingdom. If in the future the majority of the people of Northern Ireland should indicate a wish to become part of a united Ireland, the British Government would support that wish.

6. The conference agreed that a formal agreement incorporating the declarations of the British and Irish Governments would be signed at the formal stage of the conference and registered at the United Nations.

7. The conference agreed that a Council of Ireland would be set up. It would be confined to representatives of the two parts of Ireland, with appropriate safeguards for the British Government's financial and other interests. It would be comprised of a Council of Ministers with executive and harmonizing functions and a consultative role, and a Consultative Assembly with advisory and review functions. The Council of Ministers would act by unanimity, and would comprise a core of seven members of the Irish Government and an equal number of members of the Northern Ireland Executive with provision for the participation of other non-voting members of the Irish Government and the Northern Ireland Executive or Administration when matters within their departmental competence were discussed. The Council of Ministers would control the functions of the Council. The chairmanship would rotate on an agreed basis between representatives of the Irish Government and of the Northern Ireland Executive. Arrangements would be made for the location of the first meeting and the location of subsequent meetings would be determined by the Council of Ministers. The Consultative Assembly would consist of 60 members, 30 members from Dail Eireann chosen by the Dail on the basis of proportional representation by the Single Transferable Vote, and 30 members from the Northern Ireland Assembly chosen by that Assembly and also on that basis. The members of the Consultative Assembly would be paid allowances. There would be a Secretariat to the Council, which would be kept as small as might be commensurate with efficiency in the operation of the Council. The Secretariat would service the institutions of the Council and would, under the Council of Ministers, supervise the carrying out of the Executive and harmonising functions and the consultative role of the Council. The

Secretariat would be headed by a Secretary-General. Following the appointment of a Northern Ireland Executive, the Irish Government and the Northern Ireland Executive would nominate their representatives to a Council of Ministers. The Council of Ministers would then appoint a Secretary-General and decide upon the location of its permanent headquarters. The Secretary-General would be directed to proceed with the drawing up of plans for such headquarters. The Council of Ministers would also make arrangements for the recruitment of the staff of the Secretariat in a manner and on conditions which would, as far as is practicable, be consistent with those applying to public servants in the two Administrations.

8. In the context of its harmonising functions and consultative role, the Council of Ireland would undertake important work relating, for instance, to the impact of EEC [Common Market] membership. . . . In carrying out these studies, and also in determining what should be done by the Council in terms of harmonisation, the objectives to be borne in mind would include the following:

   i. To achieve the best utilisation of scarce skills, expertise and resources;

  ii. To avoid, in the interests of economy and efficiency, unnecessary duplication of effort; and

iii. To ensure complementary rather than competitive effort where this is to the advantage of agriculture, commerce and industry.

In particular, these studies would be directed to identifying, for the purposes of executive action by the Council of Ireland, suitable aspects of activities in the following broad fields:

  a) Exploitation, conservation and development of natural resources and the environment;

  b) Agricultural matters (including agricultural research, animal health and operational aspects of the common agriculture policy), forestry and fisheries;

  c) Cooperative ventures in the field of trade and industry;

  d) Electricity generation;

  e) Tourism;

  f) Roads and transport;

g) Advisory services in the field of public health;

h) Sport, culture and the arts.

It would be for the Oireachtas [Southern Parliament] and the Northern Ireland Assembly to legislate from time to time as to the extent of functions to be devolved to the Council of Ireland. Where necessary, the British Government will cooperate in this devolution of functions. Initially, the functions to be vested would be those identified in accordance with the procedures set out above and decided, at the formal stage of the conference, to be transferred.

9. (i) During the initial period following the establishment of the Council, the revenue of the Council would be provided by means of grants from the two Administrations in Ireland toward agreed projects and budgets, according to the nature of the service involved. . . .

(iii) It was agreed that the cost of the Secretariat of the Council of Ireland would be shared equally. . . .

(v) While Britain continues to pay subsidies to Northern Ireland, such payments would not involve Britain participating in the Council, it being accepted nevertheless that it would be legitimate for Britain to safeguard in an appropriate way her financial involvement in Northern Ireland.

10. It was agreed by all parties that persons committing crimes of violence, however motivated, in any part of Ireland should be brought to trial irrespective of the part of Ireland in which they are located. . . .

11. It was agreed that the Council would be invited to consider in what way the principles of the European Convention on Human Rights and Fundamental Freedoms would be exercised in domestic legislation in each part of Ireland. . . .

13. It was broadly accepted that the two parts of Ireland are to a considerable extent inter-dependent in the whole field of law and order, and that the problems of political violence and identification with the police service cannot be solved without taking account of that fact. . . .

18. The conference took note of a reaffirmation by the British Government of their firm commitment to bring detention to an end in Northern Ireland for all sections of the community as soon

as the security situation permits, and noted also that the Secretary of State for Northern Ireland hopes to be able to bring into use his statutory powers of selective release in time for a number of detainees to be released before Christmas.

19. The British Government stated that, in the light of the decisions reached at the conference, they would now seek the authority of Parliament to devolve full powers to the Northern Ireland Executive and Northern Ireland Assembly as soon as possible; the formal appointment of the Northern Ireland Executive would then be made.

British Information Services press release, 10 December 1973.

A PROPOSED UNITED NATIONS SOLUTION (1972)

The present crisis in Northern Ireland would logically be a subject for action by the Security Council because it is the United Nations organ that has the "primary responsibility for the maintenance of international peace and security." The Council's peace-keeping function is exercised by two means. First, it must seek a pacific settlement of any international dispute that is likely to endanger international peace and security. Failing this first goal, the Council is empowered to take enforcement action.

Chapter VI of the Charter sets forth the various means by which the Council may assist in the peaceful settlement of disputes and, as Article 33 makes clear, the methods of Chapter VI are supplementary to those methods traditionally established in international law and which the parties must "first of all" utilize as appropriate. These traditional means of settling disputes include negotiation, inquiry, mediation, conciliation, arbitration, judicial settlement, resort to regional agencies or arrangements, or "other peaceful means of their own choice." If the parties do not take appropriate steps to settle the dispute, however, this does not mean that the Security Council is barred from taking action. Article 33 specifically states: "The Security Council shall, when it deems necessary, call upon the parties to settle their dispute by such means."

The following have a right to submit disputes to the Council: the Assembly (Articles 11 and 12), the Secretary-General (Article 99), member States (Article 35(1)), and nonmember States (Article 35(2)). The United States, therefore, as a member State and a permanent member of the Security Council, could request the President of the Security Council to convene an urgent meeting of the Council and then submit the Northern Ireland dispute before the Council.

Once the dispute is submitted, however, it is not automatically placed on the Council's agenda. The question of whether or not to place the matter on the agenda is a procedural question requiring a majority of nine votes out of the fifteen. The United States should be able to gain the support of eight other Security Council members on this question. Once the issue is placed on the agenda, however, the question of competence still remains to be decided. The Council may decide, after considering the matter, that the dispute is not an "international" one. In other words, it may decide that it is precluded from exercising any jurisdiction by virtue of the clause in Article 2(7) asserting that "nothing contained in the present Charter shall authorize the United Nations to intervene in matters which are essentially within the domestic jurisdiction of any State or shall require the Members to submit such matters to settlement. . . ." The issue of competence is also a procedural matter requiring the affirmative votes of nine members but Great Britain could not vote on the issue because it is the member complained against. In addition, the Council may invite the parties to the dispute to participate in the discussion. The United States could, therefore, invite the Irish Republic to participate in the discussion.

The argument that Article 2(7) prevents the United Nations from acting on an "internal" matter has not stopped that Organization from investigating apartheid in South Africa and taking action during the Cyprus crisis.

The reaction of the United Nations to the outbreak of violence between Greek Cypriot and Turkish Cypriot communities in December, 1963, particularly reveals the potential for United Nations action despite Article 2(7). Great Britain tried unsuccessfully for two months to secure agreement on the replacement of this tripartite force by first a NATO force and then a Commonwealth force. Finally, Britain abandoned these attempts and, on February 15th, requested a meeting of the Security Council, proposing that a United Nations peace-keeping force should be established. On March 4, 1964, the Council unanimously adopted a resolution recommending "the creation, with the consent of the Government of Cyprus, of a United Nations peace-keeping force in Cyprus." It is important to note that the preamble of the Council resolution refers to the situation as "likely to threaten international peace and security" and not as an actual threat to international peace and security. This suggests that when a dispute is likely to threaten international peace, as is not the case in Northern Ireland, Article 2(7) cannot prevent the Security Council from taking action. The factual similarity between the Cyprus crisis and the present dispute in the Northern Ireland situation is striking.

Just as in Cyprus, the dispute in Northern Ireland is primarily between two conflicting communities and only second-arily between sovereign states, namely Great Britain and the Republic of Ireland. In addition, the government of Cyprus, led by President Makarios, exclusively represented the Greek Cypri-ots and was openly hostile to the Turkish Cypriots, a situation closely paralleled by the Stormont government in Northern Ireland. Also, just as the representatives of the minority in Northern Ireland refuse to participate in a political system designed to perpetuate the complete control of the Unionists, so the Turkish Cypriot members of the Cabinet resigned in December, 1963.

The United Nations force provided a moderating influence because it never associated itself with the official view of the Government that the Turkish Cypriots constituted a rebellious, unlawful group. A United Nations force in Northern Ireland could, likewise, be a genuinely neutral force for peace, a capacity that the British troops cannot or will not fulfill. The British realized this fact in Cyprus when they called for United Nations action. The British again admitted the need for a restrictive interpretation of Article 2(7) on October 14, 1968, when the British Secretary of State for Foreign and Commonwealth Affairs stated before the General Assembly:

Article 56 of the Charter makes it clear that no country can say that the human rights of its citizens are an exclusively domestic matter. A country that denies its citizens the basic human rights is by virtue of Article 56 in breach of an international obligation.

For Great Britain to argue now that the violence in Northern Ireland is strictly an internal matter contradicts both its actions in the Cyprus affair and its officially stated position. . . .

In order for the Council to take affirmative action, such as exercising its power to investigate under Article 34, however, a non-procedural vote is required. In other words, not only is a majority of nine votes required, but there must also be the concurrence of the five permanent members — the United States of America, Union of Soviet Socialist Republics, Great Britain, France, and China. Great Britain, therefore, has a veto power over any decision to investigate the situation in Northern Ireland. If the domestic dissent in Britain continues to mount against her policy in Northern Ireland, however, and cost in lives and money remains at the present overwhelming level, then Great Britain may find it in her own best interest to permit some level of United Nations intervention in Northern Ireland. Great Britain came around to that view in Cyprus, and she may be likely to do so again.

Statement by Kenneth McCallion, Fordham University School of Law, to U.S. House of Representatives, in *Hearings before the Subcommittee on Europe of the Committee of Foreign Affairs*, 92d Congress, 2d sess. Feb. 28 and 29 and Mar. 1, 1972, pp. 512-13.

REDRAWING THE BORDER AND DEPORTING THE CATHOLIC MINORITY (1974)

SIR, As there is still no prospect of peace in Northern Ireland, and as the main cause of the trouble appears to be the existence in that province of two irreconcilable communities, could we not solve the problem by providing for such large-scale resettlement of the population as would give every person the choice of remaining a citizen of the United Kingdom, or of becoming a resident citizen of the Irish Republic? The terms of this solution, which would include an adjustment of the present frontier, would of course have to be agreed by the main parties concerned — the Westminster and Dublin Government, and the elected representatives of the two communities in Northern Ireland. I suggest something on the following lines:

1. Those predominantly Roman Catholic areas of Northern Ireland which lie adjacent to the present frontier, to become part of the territory of the Irish Republic. The new frontier to be delineated by a United Nations Commission.

2. The remaining territory of Northern Ireland to become an integral part of the United Kingdom, on the same terms as Scotland or Wales. The Irish Republic to recognize the new status of Northern Ireland, and to amend its constitution accordingly.

3. Roman Catholics residing within the new borders of Northern Ireland to be given the choice of remaining there, as United Kingdom citizens, or of settling permanently in the Irish Republic, as Irish citizens. In the latter event, a generous resettlement grant to be paid by the British Government.

Similarly, Protestants residing in the newly-transferred Catholic areas to be given the choice of settling within the new borders of Northern Ireland. In this instance, resettlement grants to be paid by the Irish Government.

Such a scheme would be attended with enormous, but not insuperable difficulties. Its adoption would, I think, put an end to the present campaign of violence; the IRA fish could not survive long in a wholly loyalist sea. And are there any other non-violent options open? I think not.

The cost? This would not be excessive, by present-day standards. Even if the entire Catholic population of Northern Ireland decided to move to the Republic, and each family were given a resettlement grant of £5,000, the total cost to the Exchequer would not exceed the loss on Concorde.

The main objectors to the scheme would be those

Republicans who still cherish hopes of a united Ireland. But these hopes are based on a fallacy — that there is, or can be, a united Irish nation or people. There are in fact two peoples in Ireland, who have been polarized by history into a total antipathy. They do not possess the vestige of a common loyalty, let alone a common patriotism. They worship in different churches, attend different schools, sing different songs, observe different customs, cherish different traditions, applaud different heroes, and follow different flags; if their leaders had their way, they would play different games and speak different languages.

There is not the slightest chance of the two nations combining in the foreseeable future, on any basis or on any terms; the hundreds of "sectarian" murders afford a grim and ample proof of this. Even the most rabid of Republicans will sooner or later have to acknowledge this unpalatable fact.

Why not now?

Yours faithfully,
R. A. BRUCE

The Times, 29 April 1974.

SCENARIOS FOR THE FUTURE: THE BEST AND WORST ALTERNATIVES

The main alternative models for the future of this problem that now seem possible are these:

A   The 'benign' model:

The offensive of the Provisional IRA will falter and fail as a result of the increasingly hostile mood of the Catholic people; the 'water' poisoning the 'fish.' The internees will be released and internment without trial will be ended. Protestant demonstrations against this will be containable (because of the cessation of the Provisional offensive). The end of internment will permit the Catholic elected representatives to enter into serious discussion with the British Minister (Mr. Whitelaw or his successor). The end of IRA hostilities will permit the Protestant elected representatives to enter into similar discussions. This process will lead to discussions between the elected representatives of the two communities, with the British representative in essentially an arbitral role. Out of these discussions will emerge new structures with which both communities can live. These will include a thorough reform of local government, leaving any sizeable block composed of either community in charge of its own local affairs. Local affairs will include local police. A central police authority, responsible to a joint commission, will see to the recruitment, training and payment of the local forces, and will also dispose of a central police reserve, adequate to prevent one 'ghetto' being used as a base for attack on another. The British Army will be withdrawn from all responsibility for policing. As security begins to return, the British Government will invest in a massive reconstruction programme, involving major public works projects in the high unemployment (principally Catholic and Western) areas. Dublin will be invited, and will agree, to contribute to such a programme and will invite the friends of Ireland in America to do likewise. Religious discrimination in job appointments will be progressively eliminated (immediately in relation to new jobs created). Catholics will be convinced that their major grievances are being disposed of; Protestants convinced that the ending of these practices does not entail the end of the world, i.e., Catholic power over Protestants. The Dublin government will affirm its willingness to co-operate without reservation with a Northern Ireland so reconstructed and — while not abandoning an aspiration to eventual unity by free consent — will drop all 'we must have unity' propaganda.

The above is not a 'blueprint'; simply a rough sketch of the *kind* of benign evolution that could take place if the Provisional offensive definitely stopped.

If . . .

B   The malignant model:

The Provisional offensive will continue (possibly with a limited 'tactical' interruption) and even escalate. It will provoke an escalating Protestant counter-offensive including the murder of prominent Catholics, followed by retaliatory murders of Protestants. This will be followed by massed Protestant assaults on Catholic ghettoes. Some of these will be contained by the Army, some will break through. Where breakthroughs occur, the only defence the Catholics will have will be the IRA. In these conditions the IRA regains control over the ghettoes in question and can continue its activities indefinitely. The British Army comes under armed attack from both communities. With increasing casualties and no solution in sight, the British public clearly favours a policy of withdrawal. A British Government announces its agreement to the unity of Ireland, for which it receives many telegrams of congratulation from America, and urgent private messages of alarm from Dublin. The British Government, indicating that the policing of a united Ireland is a matter for the Irish Government, terminates its peace-keeping role and begins a withdrawal of its troops. Mass meetings of loyalists in Belfast acclaim 'no surrender.' An official mission from Dublin to negotiate a 'federal solution' is unable to move outside the Catholic areas of Belfast. Armed Loyalists move *en masse* into these ghettoes to get rid of the IRA once and for all, to lynch the Dublin emissaries, and to punish the Catholics generally. Thousands of Catholics are killed and scores of thousands fly south in terror: thus the water and the fish go down the drain together, from the eastern part of Northern Ireland. In the western and southern parts, Catholics start killing Protestants, and Protestants fly north and east. With or without orders from the Dublin government, the Irish army takes over in Newry, Derry and Strabane, and surrounding Catholic areas. Its efforts to penetrate the Protestant hinterland are held off, or beaten back. The Taoiseach appeals to the United Nations for technical assistance in the form of military aid. The Security Council is unable to agree.

As United Nations intervention bringing about the final unity of Ireland is one of the many illusions which bedevils this situation it may be well to dispose of it here. Why should the Security Council *not* agree to such a request from Ireland — since its accession to an identical request from the Government of the Congo in 1960 is a strict precedent, though not an altogether reassuring one? The reasons are many but the basic one is that

Britain is a permanent member of the Security Council, with
right of 'veto,' and that no conceivable British government —
least of all one that was having to face the predictable consequences of such a withdrawal — could agree to a form of United
Nations assistance which would necessarily entail 'the armed
coercion of Britishers by foreigners.' The Soviet Union and China
would loudly urge compliance with the Dublin government's
appeal: this would probably tilt the other two permanent
members, the United States and France, in favour of the British
view. In these conditions — i.e. as long as the coercion of
Protestant Ulster was a possibility in view — the Security Council
would certainly stall: that is, it would call for a cease-fire, send a
team of observers and adjourn. Later, perhaps not much later,
when the two sides, dead-locked, agreed to a cease-fire, agreement
could be found for a United Nations force to patrol the cease-fire
line: the new border.

Ireland would be left, once more, with two States, but of even
more virulent shades of green and orange than before. The
Orange State would be smaller than before — probably about
four counties — but would be homogeneously Protestant, without the tiniest Catholic crack or crevice for a new IRA to take root
in. The Green State with its massive ingestion of embittered and
displaced Ulster Catholics, would be an uncongenial environment for Protestants, most of whom would probably leave. A tiny
minority would probably remain in order to proclaim from time
to time how well treated they were and how non-sectarian
everything was compared with the terrible conditions prevailing
to the North.

Both states would be under right-wing governments,
scruffily militarist and xenophobe in character. The principal
cultural activities would be funerals, triumphal parades. commemorations, national days of mourning, and ceremonies of
rededication to the memory of those who died for Ireland/for
Ulster.

Conor Cruise O'Brien, *States of Ireland* (New York: Pantheon,
1972), pp. 298-301.

Further Reading

This section is not intended to be a comprehensive bibliography of the Ulster problem and its historical background, or a list of works consulted in preparing this book. Rather, it contains suggestions for further investigation, chosen not solely for their scholarly importance but also because they are enjoyable reading.

The best *Short History of Ireland* (New York: Harper and Row, 1968) is by J. C. Beckett. Maire and Conor Cruise O'Brien's *Concise History of Ireland* (London: Thames and Hudson, 1972) is an erudite and well-illustrated introduction to Ireland's history.

General source books on Irish history include James Carty, *Ireland: A Documentary Record* (Dublin: Fallon, 1949-51; 3 vols.), M. J. MacManus, *Irish Cavalcade, 1550-1850* (London: Macmillan, 1939), and, with its constitutional emphases, E. Curtis and R. B. McDowell, *Irish Historical Documents* (London: Methuen, 1943).

The standard *Ireland under the Tudors* and *Ireland under the Stuarts* are by Richard Bagwell, first published between 1885 and 1919. Holland Press of London reprinted this six-volume series in 1963. Far briefer are D. B. Quinn, *The Elizabethans and the Irish* (Ithaca, N. Y.: Cornell University Press, 1966), and Grenfell Morton, *Elizabethan*

Ireland (London: Longmans, 1971). Henry Morely, *Ireland under Elizabeth and James I* (London: Carisbrooke Library [vol X], 1889), is a useful reprint of contemporary English descriptions of Ireland, including those by Edmund Spenser, Sir John Davies, and Fynes Moryson.

George Hill's *Historical Account of the Plantation in Ulster at the Commencement of the Seventeenth Century, 1608-1620* (Belfast: M'Gaw and Co., 1877), the standard work on the topic, was reprinted in 1970 by the Irish University Press. In *Hell or Connaught: The Cromwellian Colonisation of Ireland, 1652-1660* (New York: St. Martins, 1975), Peter Berresford Ellis deals dispassionately with one of the bloodiest decades in Irish history.

During the next two centuries three events shaped Irish history: the Revolution of 1688, the Rising of 1798, and the Great Famine of the 1840s. Of the first event there is no work worth mentioning, an omission that is more than compensated for by Thomas F. Pakenham's *The Year of Liberty: The Story of the Great Irish Rebellion of 1798* (London: Hodder and Stoughton, 1969) and Cecil Woodham Smith's *The Great Hunger: Ireland 1845-9* (London: Hamish Hamilton, 1962).

Andrew Boyd's *Holy War in Belfast* (New York: Evergreen, 1969) is a good description of the violent — and very familiar — rioting against the Home Rule movement of the late nineteenth century. In his most readable and provocative *The Strange Death of Liberal England* (London: Constable and Co., 1936), George Dangerfield argues that the Home Rule struggle and Unionist reaction were part of a wider malaise that gripped pre-1914 Britain. While not accepting Dangerfield's thesis, though sharing his literary skill, A. T. Q. Stewart takes the story of Ireland up to partition in *The Ulster Crisis* (London: Faber, 1969).

For the current troubles, A. J. Baker's *Bloody Ulster* (New York: Ballantine, 1973) is a short and copiously illustrated introduction. The *Sunday Times'* "Insight Report," *Ulster* (Harmondsworth: Penguin, 1972), though a piece of "instant journalism," is the best description of the years up to internment.

Government documents are an invaluable source of information. Among the more important British government reports are those chaired by Lord Cameron, *Disturbances in Northern Ireland* (Belfast: Cmnd. 532, 1969); by Lord Hunt, *Police in Northern Ireland* (Belfast: Cmnd. 535, 1969); by Sir Edmund Compton, *Allegations against the Security Forces of Physical Brutality* (London: Cmnd. 4823, 1971); and by Lord Diplock, *Legal Procedures to Deal with Terrorist Activities* (London: Cmnd. 5185, 1972).

The three-day report *Hearings before the Subcommittee on Europe of the Committee of Foreign Affairs* (House of Representatives 92d Congress, 2d sess., Feb. 28 and 29 and Mar. 1, 1972), is a mine of information, most of it from a Nationalist point of view.

Two excellently illustrated books which· describe the military operations of the two sides are P. Michael O'Sullivan's *Patriot Graves: Resistance in Ireland* (Chicago: Follett, 1972) and David Barzilay's *The British Army in Ulster* (Belfast: Century Service, 1973).

Personal memoirs provide firsthand reports — as well as justifications — of their authors' actions. Prime Minister Terence O'Neill has written his *Autobiography* (London: Rupert Hart Davies, 1972), while his *bête noire*, Bernadette Devlin, has described her early life in *The Price of My Soul* (New York: Knopf, 1973). In *To Take Up Arms: My Year with the IRA Provisionals* (New York: Viking, 1973) Maria McGuire describes how she joined the IRA and, sickened by the killing, opted out. James Callaghan, the Home Secretary, describes the troubles from the British government's point of view in *A House Divided: The Dilemma of Northern Ireland* (London: Collins, 1973), while Conor Cruise O'Brien provides a Southern perspective in *States of Ireland* (New York: Pantheon, 1972). In the aptly titled *In Holy Terror* (London: Faber and Faber, 1974), Simon Winchester records his stint as a newspaper correspondent in Belfast.

A fascinating book, which is free from the biases of personal memoirs, is Richard Roses' *Goverment without Consensus: An Irish Perspective* (London: Faber and Faber, 1971). Rose uses sophisticated polling techniques to discover the social and political attitudes of the people of Northern Ireland just before the outbreak of the current troubles.

Richard R. Deutsch, *Northern Ireland, 1921-1974: A Select Bibliography* (New York and London: Garland, 1975) is a most useful listing of works, valuably annotated. It complements his two-volume *Northern Ireland, 1968–1973: A Chronology of Events* (Belfast: Blackstaff, 1973–1974).

One element of the Ulster crisis and its background can never be fully gained from books: the songs of rebellion and loyalism. The records of the Clancy Brothers and Tommy Makem are especially recommended.

Index